Online

Helping you get to grips with online learning, this book contains a wealth of practical tips and strategies that will make studying online easier.

Covering the advantages of online learning as well as the problems you might face, this book provides tried and tested advice to help you overcome those difficulties so that you can work to the best of your abilities. Identifying techniques designed specifically for studying online, this key guide explores topics and methods such as:

- the differences between traditional and online study, preparing for online study as well as planning and organising;
- making sole working a collaborative and shared experience;
- reading online, online notetaking, using study forums, using video, collaboration, and coping with online exams;
- understanding the possible effects on mental and physical health and how to cope with the distractions the virtual world can bring while taking care of your mental and physical health.

With step-by-step instructions for each of the techniques, as well as guidance on using online study software to the best effect, this must-have student companion provides tips and tricks to make university distance studying both effective and enjoyable.

Graham Jones B.Sc. (Hons), B.A. (Hons), Adv.Dip.Ed., MBPsS, M.Sc., M.Ed., FHEA, CMBE, FPSA is a Senior Lecturer and Programme Director for undergraduate degrees in the Business School at the University of Buckingham, UK. He is also an Associate Lecturer at The Open University. Graham has been teaching online since 1999, when he was one of a pioneering group of academics who started to use the Internet to deliver courses. He has more than 22 years of experience in teaching online and has supported several thousand students with their online studies. As a psychologist who specialises in understanding how people use the Internet, he is ideally placed to write this book.

Routledge Study Skills

Writing a Postgraduate Thesis or Dissertation
Tools for Success
Michael Hammond

Studying Online
Succeeding through Distance Learning at University
Graham Jones

For more information about this series, please visit: https://www.routledge.com/Routledge-Study-Skills/book-series/ROUTLEDGESS

Studying Online

Succeeding through Distance
Learning at University

Graham Jones

Routledge
Taylor & Francis Group

LONDON AND NEW YORK

Cover image: © Getty Images

First published 2023
by Routledge
4 Park Square, Milton Park, Abingdon, Oxon OX14 4RN

and by Routledge
605 Third Avenue, New York, NY 10158

Routledge is an imprint of the Taylor & Francis Group, an informa business

© 2023 Graham Jones

British Library Cataloguing-in-Publication Data
A catalogue record for this book is available from the British Library

Library of Congress Cataloging-in-Publication Data
Names: Jones, Graham, 1956– author.
Title: Studying online : succeeding through distance learning at university /
   Graham Jones.
Description: Abingdon, Oxon ; New York, NY : Routledge, 2022. |
   Series: Routledge study skills | Includes bibliographical references and index.
Identifiers: LCCN 2021061820 (print) | LCCN 2021061821 (ebook) |
   ISBN 9781032195384 (hardback) | ISBN 9781032195391 (paperback) |
   ISBN 9781003259695 (ebook)
Subjects: LCSH: Education, Higher—Effect of technological innovations on. |
   Web-based instruction. | Study skills.
Classification: LCC LB2395.7 .J66 2022 (print) | LCC LB2395.7 (ebook) |
   DDC 378.1/7344678—dc23/20211221
LC record available at https://lccn.loc.gov/2021061820
LC ebook record available at https://lccn.loc.gov/2021061821

ISBN: 978-1-032-19538-4 (hbk)
ISBN: 978-1-032-19539-1 (pbk)
ISBN: 978-1-003-25969-5 (ebk)

DOI: 10.4324/9781003259695

Typeset in Warnock Pro
by Apex CoVantage, LLC

Contents

Illustrations

▶ FIGURES

▶ TABLES

Acknowledgements

Like all books, this one hasn't been possible without the support of other people. First, I want to thank all my students who have inspired me to write this book. I would like to thank them for sharing their difficulties with online studies and for being so honest about what works and does not work for them. Their questions and ideas have been very helpful indeed. My colleagues at the University of Buckingham and the Open University have also helped me with ideas and supported me throughout the writing of this book, so they deserve a thank you too. Three people in particular provided support for my idea before I'd even started writing. These are Tim Durkin, Dr Lynda Shaw, and Jela Webb, who all provided encouragement. I would also like to thank Professor Nigel Adams, who introduced me to the team at Routledge. Finally, I am very grateful to my editors at Routledge, Sue Cope, Sarah Hyde and Zoe Thomson, who have been a tremendous support, as has Akshara Dafre, Editorial Assistant.

Introduction

The number of students taking online courses is dramatically increasing. In 2004 only 15 per cent of students took any form of an online class; in 2020, that rose to almost 100 per cent. The COVID pandemic forced almost all universities and colleges to teach exclusively online. Students had to cope with an entirely new way of learning that most had not previously encountered. They had to adapt quickly, and for many, it was a struggle. I spoke with several students who were finding it difficult to make the transfer from face-to-face learning to online studies. It was my discussions with these students that triggered the initial idea for this book.

Now, with universities returning to face-to-face lectures, they have still retained a considerable amount of online teaching. Using the Internet to deliver classes has several advantages for universities and students alike. Students can learn at their own pace, while universities can deliver classes to larger groups of individuals. With online teaching, lecturers can be more creative and make the delivery more engaging than face-to-face classes. In turn, this increases the involvement of students who become more interested and motivated as a result.

However, studying online is different to classroom study. College and university students who are not on campus, but learning via the Internet, need to be more self-disciplined and self-motivated. They have to be more organised, cope with more distractions and be flexible in their communications with other students. These are skills that are not required to the same degree in traditional, in-person study situations.

This book explores what those studying online need to do so that they can genuinely benefit from being distance learners. *Studying*

Online takes you through the steps needed to make the most of Internet-based studying. You will learn what you need to do to get the best possible marks and have an enjoyable online university experience. Whether you are studying entirely online or are using Internet learning as part of a traditional university programme, this book will help.

The book begins with Chapter 1, looking at how online education differs from face-to-face teaching and why that matters. The Chapter explores the advantages and disadvantages of studying online and highlights some of the issues discussed in the remainder of the book.

Chapter 2 considers what you need to have in place for effective online study. It looks at the technical equipment you will need, such as hardware and software. This chapter also discusses the need to prepare your study space and negotiate with the rest of the household so they can let you study in peace.

With online study, much of your reading material will be provided in the form of ebooks and other web-based documents. Chapter 3 considers the differences between reading online and in print. The chapter discusses the need for more regular breaks when you are reading on-screen. There is also a section in this chapter discussing whether you should print your reading materials. Plus, Chapter 3 also considers the use of audiobooks as part of your learning.

Chapter 4 is about taking notes. This chapter discusses the various notetaking systems available to online students. It looks at the differences between taking paper notes and digital notes. There is also a discussion of online notebook systems such as OneNote from Microsoft. In addition, this chapter looks at the annotation of digital documents for computers, tablets, and mobiles.

In Chapter 5, you will be able to read about the value of online study forums. Many educational establishments use these study forums and group discussions as part of each module. This chapter investigates how they work and shows how to get the best out of them.

Chapter 6 is all about online videos. Most lectures will be available as recorded or live, "streamed" videos. This chapter considers the best ways to use online video. There is also more detail in this chapter about webcams and video setups. As an online student, you will be taking part in online video sessions, so this chapter helps you ensure that you are set up to make the most of these.

Collaboration with other students in group work is an essential part of university study. So, Chapter 7 discusses the various forms of online collaboration you can use to work with other students in group projects. This chapter discusses the value and use of social media for connecting with other students. It also considers how you can engage in "informal" learning through online collaboration.

In Chapter 8, you will find advice on how to make effective presentations online. You will need to make several presentations as an online student. These will range from presenting your ideas in tutorials to formal presentations that are assessed. However, making presentations on a computer, distant from everyone else, requires different approaches compared with presenting face-to-face. So, this chapter explains what you need to do to make the most of online presenting as a student.

Chapter 9 is all about assessments. Inevitably you will be assessed. However, with all your assignments and exams online, you will need to prepare and plan differently from traditional class-based assessments. This chapter looks at the variety of online assessments you could face and explains how to be organised for online assessment. You will also read in this Chapter how to cope with online proctored examinations.

In Chapter 10, you will find advice on coping with the myriad distractions that face online students. Some are obvious, such as social media notifications. However, others are not immediately obvious such as the social activity in a household. This Chapter also looks at software that can help reduce distractions. In addition, Chapter 10 looks at other methods of keeping focused, including timer devices and even signs to go on the study room door.

Finally, Chapter 11 looks at your well-being while studying online. Sitting at your computer for many hours is not good for your mental or physical health. This chapter looks at various issues, including posture, eye problems and sleep, that are all associated with long hours sitting at a computer.

Throughout the book, you will find several "Quick tips" within each chapter that highlight some of the critical actions you can take to help improve your online studying. Also, at the end of each chapter, a list of "Practical tips" summarises some of the important actions you need to take if you want to make the most of your online studies.

Each chapter includes research evidence to support the points that are being made. A full list of references to the sources is provided at the end of each chapter.

Finally, I have created a website to accompany this book – https:// studyingonline.tips. There are several references to the site throughout the book. On the website, you will see up-to-date listings of software and other useful resources mentioned in the book.

Part I

Getting ready for online study

1 What is different about online study?

At the end of 1999, I was simultaneously involved with two new daunting activities. I became a father when my son was born in November 1999. As any new parent will tell you, that's a rather frightening time as you become responsible for a new life. At the same time, I started to teach on a ground-breaking course at the UK's Open University, which was taught partially online. It felt like I was some kind of revolutionary explorer, helping bring two types of new life into the world.

The Open University course was called "You, Your Computer and the Internet". It was the first to include online teaching, learning, and assessment. It attracted 10,000 students in its first year showing just how much interest there was in the topic and the new way of studying online (Open University, 2018).

The students who enrolled were keen to understand the burgeoning technology and its potential impact on the world. They were also interested in discovering the new way of learning using online conference software and web pages. I remember one evening being in a classroom with a group of students at Newbury College in Berkshire, UK and hearing their excitement about being able to

DOI: 10.4324/9781003259695-2

experiment with delivering their assignments "over the Internet". These students must have felt like pioneers investigating a new land and making fresh discoveries.

A great deal has changed in the 22 years since I started teaching online. My son has grown up, and the world of online studying has changed dramatically. I am sure I have made many mistakes along the way, both as a father and an online educator. But one thing that has always been clear is my passion for finding new things shared by my son and my students. It is this desire to experiment with anything new that is leading so many students towards online studying.

▶ ONLINE LEARNING IS PERSONAL

So many students have been enthusiastic about online learning because it gives them a sense of freedom and control that isn't as obvious with traditional studying. The students back in 1999 who were pioneering the use of online conferencing software realised that they could study when they wanted in the most suitable way for them. This is an essential aspect of online learning. It can be moulded to you and the way you want to study.

Before online study – indeed even now with traditional courses – students had to attend the lectures when the timetable said so. Students on "ordinary" study programmes are forced to attend class according to the demands and requirements of the lecturer and the university. People studying the traditional way only get to do the work provided each week or when the lecturer decides to hand it out.

When you study online, you get to choose when you watch the lectures. You decide what to study, often in which order you prefer. You can personalise your studying in ways that are just not possible with traditional university courses. Indeed, the whole notion of "personalised learning" has been a dream of educators for many years. Over 60 years ago, the psychologist B.F. Skinner explored the potential use of "teaching machines" (Skinner, 1958). He demonstrated that students could learn without the presence of a teacher. Skinner was clearly ahead of his time. He predicted that "teaching machines" would be used so that students could study from home. He also suggested that these machines would help to expand education to people with disabilities. There was much interest in his work. Over the years, educational researchers have found that performance increases when learning is personalised. The more that studying is centred around the individual student's personal interests, motivations, and requirements, the better they perform in assessments.

The digital age in which we live has made the dream of personalised learning much more tangible than previously. There is still some way to go; many universities, and other educational institutions, are focused on traditional delivery methods. They are only providing truly personalised studying as an "added extra". That said, the rapid growth of online studying due to international lockdowns following the global Coronavirus pandemic in 2020–2021 triggered universities to dramatically change their offerings to students. Nowadays, students expect an element of online studying. That's because they have discovered that it gives them much more control and a personalised approach.

▶ THE FLEXIBILITY OF ONLINE LECTURES

As a university lecturer, organising the timetable is one of the most troublesome activities at the start of each term or semester. It can't be fixed, with lecturers doing the same lectures every term on the same day and time. Each year the number of students on a degree programme changes, as also happens on the individual modules. For instance, I had more than 80 students select one of the modules I was teaching in one year. The year after it was only 30. Fluctuations like this mean that each year different sized lecture theatres are needed. With the same thing happening to lecturers throughout a university, it is a major "jigsaw puzzle" putting together the timetable where rooms can be matched to class sizes. The result is that each term lecturers are often as surprised when they are teaching a subject as the students. Lecturers and students alike dread seeing one thing on their timetable – the "9 o'clock lecture". University students do not like getting up for a 9:00 am lecture. Lecturers do not like seeing this on their timetable either as they know that attendance will be low.

Enter the world of online lectures. If you want, you can watch a lesson at any time of the day or night. It is entirely up to you as a student. Lecturers also like the flexibility because they can record the lectures when convenient to them, rather than when an administrator has timetabled the event. Online learners and lecturers alike can be genuinely independent, deciding when they will deal with the lectures according to their own requirements. This appears to have a positive effect. Anecdotally, several students have told me that they prefer the online way of studying. When I checked their results, they also appeared to be gaining higher marks after switching to online studies than they were in the months beforehand. This is borne out by research. A study at Tel Aviv University found that online students "reported better understanding of the course structure, better communication with the course staff" and "higher engagement and satisfaction" (Soffer and Nachmias, 2018).

> QUICK TIP: If you have a chance to study an element of your degree online, choosing that option can improve your enjoyment of the module.

▶ ONLINE LECTURES ALLOW FOR SELF-PACING

One Wednesday morning in the middle of a term, I walked into the Sunley Lecture Theatre in the Chandos Road Building at the University of Buckingham. It's a small lecture theatre holding about 80 students, and it is at the end of a long corridor where you have to walk past several other teaching rooms. I was a little hot and bothered as I entered the lecture theatre. I had rushed to get there from the other side of the campus following a meeting that had over-run. It's an uphill walk to the building and then a long walk down the corridor. I walked into the lecture theatre a couple of minutes after the lecture should have started. I apologised to the students as I set up the lecture slides I needed. Then I noticed that instead of the 60 students I was expecting there were only about 30 present. "Where is everyone else?" I asked. It turned out that they had been called to an urgent revision session for another module they were studying. Exams were coming up for that module, and the only time available for their revision session clashed with my lecture. I thought for a moment about what I could do. After all, it was not the students' fault for missing the lesson. "Here's what I suggest", I said to the class. "What if we cancel today's lecture and I record it? That way, everyone will be able to watch it, and the students who are not here will not miss out".

The students who were in the lecture theatre thought it was a great idea. I joked with them, suggesting it meant they could get to the student union bar an hour earlier. But one of them suggested another reason. He said, "Actually, many of us prefer recorded lectures". I asked him to explain why. As he told me, there were plenty of nods of agreement from around the room. The student said that recorded lectures can be paused while notes are made or to look up definitions. "I can't pause you in the lecture theatre when you are in full stride", he said. "And if I look something up, I will have missed what you were saying. That doesn't happen with recorded lectures". He went on to add that the recorded lecture can be left unfinished, to be completed at another more convenient time. Another advantage of recorded lectures was the ease with which good notes can be made. In class, with a lecturer chatting away, students can find it tough to take effective notes. They can get back to their room and find it hard to decipher their scrawl or scratch their heads about what their "shorthand" actually meant. There is no need for rapid writing of notes or fancy shorthand systems with online recorded lectures. Instead, the notes can be taken while the lecture is paused. That means the notes can be more extensive and make more sense.

That conversation made me realise that traditional lectures are given at the pace of the lecturer rather than at the speed the student wants. Often, lecturers have to cram in a great deal of information. They only have an hour or two, and there is usually an extensive syllabus to get through. However, that doesn't allow lectures to be delivered at the pace of each individual student. Some students will want things to go more slowly than others so that they can think about what is being said. Other students will want to look up terms if they are not sure about their meaning. Either way, the recorded lecture allows the material to be delivered at the student's pace, not the lecturer's.

▶ ONLINE LECTURES LEAD TO "CHUNKING"

Another benefit of the recorded lecture is the psychological benefit of "chunking". Memory is improved when we "chunk" things together. Suppose you need to remember a series of items. It is easier to recall them if you can group several of them together, rather than trying to deal with them individually. Traditional lectures, delivered once a week, don't make that easy for students. Something learned one week might be connected to an item in previous weeks. However, with the gap between the lectures, it can be tough to make those connections. This is one reason students have to spend so much time revising for exams.

With online lectures, students can watch videos in a batch. This allows students to make connections that would not be obvious when the material is delivered separately over a more extended period. With online lectures, students can "chunk" together the content of the recordings, making it easier to recall items.

> QUICK TIP: *Watch lecture videos in small batches to help your overall understanding of the topic.*

▶ GOODBYE "CHALK AND TALK"

Traditional university lecturing has been known as "chalk and talk", even though lecturers gave up using blackboards with chalk many years ago. However, the phrase represents a style of lecturing that really should have been dispensed with a long time ago. The "chalk and talk" method of delivering lectures is where the teacher stands at the front of the class, talks "at" the students, writes things on a board, or shows slides that merely repeat what is said.

To understand why this is so outdated, it is worthwhile considering the history of universities. When these seats of learning began several hundred years ago, the professors were considered to be experts of such high regard they were somewhat distant from students. Many of the students at that time were illiterate and had to learn by having the words of the great professor read to them. The person who did this was known as the "reader" who stood at a "lectern" on which the professor's book rested. In universities today, there are still "readers" who are one rung down the academic hierarchy from a professor. There is, though, an enormous difference with today's students. These days, all the students can read, so the "readers" do not have to read the professor's work aloud.

Back in those early days of university, the professor would sit on a raised chair on the platform as the textbook's pages were read aloud by the reader. The professor was known to sit in "the chair", and even today, hundreds of years later, professors "hold the chair" of the subject for which they are an expert. In some ancient universities, such as Cambridge, there are still remnants of old lecture theatres where you can see the professor's chair and the lectern from which the reader gave the lecture.

However, if you pause and think for a while, "chalk and talk" lecturing is pretty much what was going on over 800 years ago in universities when most students could not read and had to learn by listening. In reality, this method of lecturing ought to have been abolished in the post-Victorian era, when everyone learned to read. The fact that the lecturing style has persisted tells you a lot about the speed of change in education.

The online world, though, has led to rapid change, the outdated chalk and talk method of lecturing is being abandoned. In its place has come a much more interactive style of lecturing, using a range of ways of delivering the "content" of the lecture. This makes modern online lectures more engaging than real-world chalk and talk lectures.

Modern online video lectures can include:

- Additional notes supplying background on what is being said
- Hyperlinks to extra materials, such as interviews with experts to expand on what is said in the lecture
- Walkthrough demonstrations
- Extra audio materials in the form of podcasts, for example
- Pictures and illustrations to enhance what is said in the lecture
- Interactive features, such as a quiz with instant feedback
- Games
- Three-dimensional items
- Virtual reality components.

There is so much more to the modern online lecture which helps enhance the learning experience. Done well, the best online classes make the "chalk and talk" lectures of just a couple of years ago seem like they really were from the tenth century.

▶ ONLINE LEARNING IS NOT ALL "TECHNICAL"

One of the main difficulties with studying online is the need to be technologically proficient. Even though computer usage is widespread, and many students will have been using mobile phones for a decade before starting university, there are still individuals who do not like technology or find it difficult. That can limit the benefit of online studying for some students. After all, traditional studying needs only the relatively straightforward technological requirement of pen and paper. For students to access hyperlinked background notes, additional in-depth materials, or take part in virtual reality sessions, a reasonable level of technical skills becomes a requirement. In a study at Southern Utah University, USA, it was found that a student's belief in their ability to cope with online study was directly related to their level of technology skills (Kobayashi, 2017). This suggests that students who think they are not very technical are less likely to cope with online studying, even if they are actually more technologically savvy than they realise. What was clear from this study was that despite all the technical enhancements available with online studies, most students tend to prefer what you might call "ordinary" videos. This was despite the availability of the "rich media" offered by the potential of online studying. So, as a student, you do not have to be as "technical" as you might think. You will do fine if you stick to the "ordinary" online materials.

One of the issues with online technology is our lack of knowledge or understanding about many of the features. You probably use a word processor, such as Microsoft Word or Google Docs. Microsoft Word has 1,924 different commands available (yes, I counted them ...!). How many of them do you use? If you are like most people, not many of them. In answer to a question on a Microsoft help forum about the use of Word, the company revealed that just five commands make up 32 per cent of the usage of the program. This is before you even consider the fact you can add an endless array of "macros" to add even more features to the software. The chances are you use Microsoft Word or Google Docs quite well, without knowing more than a handful of the features. It doesn't put you off using the word processor. However, when it comes to online studying, it appears that students can be put off because they feel they are not technically proficient.

> QUICK TIP: *You are more capable with technology than you think. Dive in and have a go and you will do fine. If you think you are no good with technology it becomes a self-fulfilling prophecy.*

▶ STUDYING ONLINE IS LONELY

Ever since I started teaching at the Open University, back in 1999, I have been telling students they need to be more like "traditional" university students. The students have looked at me blankly when I say that. After all, they chose to study at the Open University because they do not want to go and join a bunch of students on campus. Plus, they want the flexibility of learning at a distance. So, when I am met with those blank looks, I explain what I mean. Much of the learning in a campus-based university does not happen in the lecture theatre or the library. It occurs in the coffee shop, on the lawns, or in the student union bar. Students at traditional universities spend a great deal of time together. Indeed, they spend much more time talking with each other about their studies than they do in "contact time" with lecturers.

In the UK – along with many other countries – a degree is made up of "credits". You have to get 360 credit points to gain an honours degree. Each module or course is allocated a number of credits. Typically, a module at a British university is 20 credits. Each credit requires 10 hours of study. So, a 20-credit course is the equivalent of 200 hours of study. However, the vast majority of that time is "self-directed" learning or "guided" learning. Only about 30 hours of the 200 is spent with lecturers. For the remaining 170 hours, a student is "on their own". Some of that time will be "guided" learning, where the lecturer has suggested specific chapters of books to read, for instance. But most of it is down to the student to find out for themselves what they need to know and learn. Central to this "self-directed" learning is talking with other students. Meeting each other over coffee or chatting over an evening drink in the bar is where a lot of discussion takes place between students. This leads them to think, to look things up later, and helps them analyse the topics.

Distance learning students, such as those I teach at the Open University, do not have the possibility of meeting each other casually over a beer in the union building. As a result, anyone studying online is deprived of a central component of traditional university learning. That's why I always encourage distance learning students to form social groups and meet up as often as possible. Even if it is a monthly meal together on a Friday night, that's better than being alone. Following the lockdowns due to COVID-19, I asked students who had moved from traditional campus-based to online studies what was the main difficulty with that transition. Over 90 per cent of them said the lack of social connection and the resulting loneliness were the most significant problems.

▶ MULTIPLE COMMUNICATION METHODS DON'T HELP

When I was a student, before the advent of social media, there were two ways of communication with students. Either an announcement of something important was made in class, or a note was distributed into your "pigeonhole". This was a small box where all your post was delivered each day. If students wanted to communicate with other students, they pinned up a handwritten item on a noticeboard in the student union building or in the hall of residence. As a student, it meant I only had to attend class, check my pigeonhole each day, and look at the noticeboards every now and then. That's all I needed to do to make sure that I was fully informed about everything.

Fast forward to today when there are multiple communication methods. Students now get:

- Emails
- Messages on Moodle or Blackboard
- Announcements in administration forums
- Announcements in module forums
- Messages on collaborative systems such as Microsoft Teams or Slack
- Group messages in WhatsApp
- Individual messages on Facebook Messenger

- Web browser notifications and updates for specific services, such as online teaching videos
- Chat in team-based applications.

This is all before you even start to consider the messages students send each other on various systems, including SMS, Snapchat, or Telegram. Plus, many universities will also have physical notice-boards or even post letters out to students. It is so much more complicated to keep updated these days than when I was a student.

For people studying online, there is an added complication. They are not in the student union or the coffee bar where conversations along the lines of "Did you see that notice about ...?" occur. Individual students learning at a distance might overlook a specific communication. They don't bump into other students where a casual conversation could alert an individual to the relevant information. As a result, it is easy for distance learning students to miss seeing some messages even though the university will say, "But we sent out a notice about it". Unlike the "olden days" when I was at university, today's students have too many communication methods, which is overwhelming.

> **QUICK TIP:** *Think about the various communications methods you will use and have a plan for which kind of messages will use which method.*

▶ ONLINE STUDYING IS DISTRACTING

The biggest distraction for most young adults in a lecture theatre is that attractive individual sitting just a few rows away who they would love to get to know. Other than that, most lecture theatres are uninspiring places. Online studying, for all its flexibility, can be hugely distracting, though. You can, for instance, study in your garden or on the beach, where you can be taken away from your studies by watching butterflies or the people windsurfing. In the lecture theatre, you might doodle on your notebook, but that's about all you can do. However, once you are online, you can go off and do a host of other more exciting things, from watching the latest TikTok to checking out the latest memes on Twitter. This is all before you consider the distractions that arise from notifications and pings about messages or updates. In a study at the Faculty of Education at Kuwait University, researchers found that it was the "fear of missing out" (FOMO) that leads students to be distracted from their studies (Al-Furaih and Al-Awidi, 2021). Notifications that alert students to information mean they get distracted because they are concerned that they will miss out on something important. On the one hand, the technology is helping ensure students are well-informed. On the other hand, it leads to more distractions from studies, reducing attention and concentration. Technology is simultaneously helping and hindering online studying.

Another feature of online study that leads to distraction is the never-ending supply of information. In the past, students had their textbooks and the library. Suppose they wanted to delve deeper into a subject. In that case, they could only go as far as the available resources allowed them. However, with online studying, students can keep on searching for more and more information on a topic. They can go down long and winding routes through various web sources, delving ever deeper into a specific topic. This can take students away from the central aspect of what they should be studying. The benefit of having a never-ending library of information, thanks to the World Wide Web, is also a hindrance to students. It can distract them onto interesting items tangential to their real focus.

▶ MOTIVATION FOR STUDYING IS REDUCED ONLINE

Motivation is an essential aspect of studying. Students want to achieve their absolute best, of course. However, in traditional university settings, much of the motivation comes from competitiveness. Students will have their own goals for marks, but they always want to do better than their peers or those who they see as like themselves. In those "olden days" when I was at university, students got their work back in their pigeonholes. We would gather around those post boxes on the days when assignments were due back to retrieve our work and look at the marks. "What did you get?" was a frequent question amongst friends.

Online there is no joint collection of results. Students may get an individual email or notification. There is no chance to ask, "What did you get?" This means that an element of competition or re-assurance is more difficult to obtain, which could impact upon motivation. From the initial stages of online education in the late 1990s, the late educational psychologist, Professor Paul Pintrich from the University of Michigan, USA, established a clear link between student motivation and their success (Pintrich, 1999).

It is difficult for online students to get motivated, though. In my small study of students who had transferred from traditional classroom teaching to online-only learning, half of them said that motivation was an issue. One student said,

> *The learning is missing the essential human contact that draws and keeps your attention, and knowing everything is recorded and can be watched at your leisure can make it hard to be motivated to complete a lecture on the day, meaning there becomes a large backlog of unwatched lectures and unfinished work.*

In traditional teaching, students will see their lecturers in the coffee bar. They will bump into them in the corridors or encounter them at events around the campus. This gives them an opportunity to ask questions or just pass the time of day. Such small conversations are frequently motivational for students. However, in the online distance learning world, such ad-hoc meetings do not occur, reducing the opportunity for motivation. Online students, therefore, need to be highly self-motivated.

QUICK TIP: *If you find motivation difficult, speak to a friend. Have a chat and you will find this social contact helps motivate you.*

▶ PARTICIPATION IN ONLINE STUDY IS DIFFERENT

Often, because of higher levels of motivation with real-world learning, students find it easier to take part. They can see others around them studying – in the study areas, or in the library, for example. This gives them the incentive to learn. At home, when studying at a distance, though, there is no one else around who is studying. There are no role models. As a result, it is all too easy to reduce participation in studying when doing it online. As one student said to me, "I can easily zone out and get bored. Postponing the work to later on becomes a habit".

This is related to motivation, of course. However, there is another factor at play here. In traditional learning, participation is often directed by the academic staff. Students attend lectures, make notes, and do the follow-up reading (hopefully ...!). With online study, students are expected to direct themselves much more. There is often less opportunity for the informal direction that happens within a traditional campus-based study. As a result, participation in online studying is much more dependent upon the student themselves. Lecturers do have an influence, of course, but as research in the USA discovered, student participation can be limited by the technology and design of online courses (Vonderwell and Zachariah, 2005). Other research has shown a similar finding by demonstrating that participation is clearly related to the design of an online module (Anthony, 2012). For students, this means it is often difficult to find their way around poorly designed online modules so they might not be able to participate fully.

▶ "BLENDED LEARNING" OR THE "FLIPPED CLASSROOM"

Within the world of education, the notion of "blended learning" has been the subject of much discussion since the 1960s. The idea is that students do some face-to-face studying using traditional methods but also complete certain tasks using technology. As you can tell from much of this chapter, there are some excellent features of online studying. However, there are also several downsides making it more challenging for students to learn exclusively online. As a result, blended learning could deliver the "best of both worlds", providing advantages for both styles of studying without the associated problems.

Blended learning, as such, has been used by the Open University for over 50 years. Students received video cassette recordings of lectures in the post or watched programmes on BBC2 television in the early hours of the morning. They were also supplied with audio cassettes with lessons on them. In addition, the students would get monthly face-to-face sessions with expert tutors. They would teach them other aspects of the module or help consolidate what they had learned from the recordings. This method allowed students to benefit from the advantages of self-directed learning and gain the positive aspects of face-to-face teaching. A similar approach is used by the Khan Academy for schoolchildren around the world. This combines online learning materials with classroom teaching in a wide variety of school subjects. Research shows that children tend to perform better with this blended approach (Zengin, 2017).

Both the Open University and the Khan Academy are using the notion of blended learning known as a "flipped classroom". This is where students learn material on their own first, then they go to a classroom where that learning can be strengthened and enhanced. Universities are considering blended approaches and flipped classrooms following their enforced delivery of online learning following the Coronavirus pandemic in 2000. Having invested in online delivery technology, they are reluctant to give it up entirely. For many university students, a blended approach or a flipped classroom is going to be the norm. However, suppose your modules are entirely online with no blended or flipped approach. In that case, you will need to consider carefully how you will limit the disadvantages of online learning. The rest of this book will provide you with several ideas about how to do that.

PRACTICAL TIPS

- **Make a plan.** Because online learning can be so personal and individual, you should develop a study plan to suit yourself. You do not have to follow the suggested way of studying if it does not serve you. See Chapter 2 for more advice.
- **Get to grips with the technology.** Familiarise yourself with all the technical requirements. You don't have to know everything. You don't know everything about your word processor, after all. But get to grips with the basics as it will improve your positive feelings about the technology. Those feelings are linked to effectiveness. See Chapter 2 for more advice.
- **Form a social group.** Meet up with people regularly. Even if you think there is nothing to discuss, a coffee and a chat will help trigger ideas. This will also help with your motivation. See Chapter 5 for more advice.
- **Set up routines to check communications.** There are so many communications systems available it is difficult to keep up. If you establish a habit of checking all possible sources for messages, you won't miss out. See Chapter 11 for more details.

► REFERENCES

Al-Furaih, S.A.A. and Al-Awidi, H.M. (2021) 'Fear of Missing Out (FoMO) among Undergraduate Students in Relation to Attention Distraction and Learning Disengagement in Lectures', *Education and Information Technologies*, 26(2), pp. 2355–2373.

Anthony, K.V. (2012) 'Analyzing the Influences of Course Design and Gender on Online Participation', *Online Journal of Distance Learning Administration*, XII(III).

Kobayashi, M. (2017) 'Students' Media Preferences in Online Learning', *Turkish Online Journal of Distance Education*, 18(3), pp. 4–14.

Open University (2018) '50 Objects for 50 Years. No 37. Conferencing Software', *History of the OU*. Available at: www.open.ac.uk/blogs/ History-of-the-OU/?p=3081 (Accessed: 16 August 2021).

Pintrich, P.R. (1999) 'The Role of Motivation in Promoting and Sustaining Self-Regulated Learning', *International Journal of Educational Research*, 31(6), pp. 459–470.

Skinner, B.F. (1958) 'Teaching Machines', *Science*, 128(3330), pp. 969–977.

Soffer, T. and Nachmias, R. (2018) 'Effectiveness of Learning in Online Academic Courses Compared with Face-to-Face Courses in Higher Education', *Journal of Computer Assisted Learning*, 34(5), pp. 534–543.

Vonderwell, S. and Zachariah, S. (2005) 'Factors that Influence Participation in Online Learning', *Journal of Research on Technology in Education*, 38(2), pp. 213–230.

Zengin, Y. (2017) 'Investigating the Use of the Khan Academy and Mathematics Software with a Flipped Classroom Approach in Mathematics Teaching', *Journal of Educational Technology & Society*, 20(2), pp. 89–100.

2 Preparing for online study

Studying online provides you with great flexibility, as discussed in Chapter 1. However, that flexibility can also pose you with questions that you haven't needed to answer before. If you have studied traditionally at a university, you do not have to decide where and how you will learn. The university itself has made several decisions in advance, forcing you to study in a particular way. This was clear when I helped my son move into his accommodation at the Fallowfield Campus when he started at the University of Manchester in 2018. The room had a study bench that went across the width of the bedroom in front of the window. There were bookshelves on one side of this desk arrangement. On the other side was a pinboard. There was a desk lamp and a chair. Everything was in place for my son to just sit down and get on with his studies. As I drove the 200 miles home after waving him off onto his new adventure, I realised how little had changed since I went to university. When I arrived at the Cathedral Court accommodation at the University of Surrey, my room had a desk with bookshelves above and a pinboard to the side. I was also given a chair and table lamp. Research conducted at Moscow State University (Popov, 2018) showed that student accommodation has been pretty much the same since the ninth century – though lights wouldn't have been electric back

DOI: 10.4324/9781003259695-3

then, of course ...! For hundreds of years, universities have been setting out how students will study.

Even if you do not want to study in your bedroom (and many students don't), traditional universities provide alternatives. You can use the library or study areas within faculties or school buildings. Some of the more up-to-date campuses have "study pods". These are small cubicles that are for a student on their own or for small groups. These pods range from simple items to designer-style options or small rooms in garden areas, for instance. However, the university has decided what you need to study. Ultimately, the study pods are the same – desk, light, seat, computer access. Students don't really get much choice.

However, studying online provides students with a range of options they have not needed to consider before. Furthermore, if you are studying online, you now need to think about all the possibilities previously worked out and provided for you by the university. Studying online means you have to make all the decisions yourself, which would have been made for you with traditional study.

▶ WHERE WILL YOU STUDY?

Studying online means that you get the option to choose where to study. You can study from anywhere because you are not tied to one place. You can study from any room in your house or study from the garden if you have one. If you don't have a garden, why not study in the local park, if the weather is good? Or you could study in a nearby library or your favourite coffee shop. Some people even study from the beach.

In 2020 when the Coronavirus pandemic forced students to study at a distance I remember speaking with one of my students via Microsoft Teams. I noticed that he was somewhere relatively sunny, and he was high up on a balcony. "Where are you?" I asked because I was curious. I knew where the student lived, and he certainly wasn't on campus in the rather dreary weather we were experiencing at the time ...! "I am in Dubai", he said. He had worked out that with a cheap flight and a good deal on Airbnb, he could cancel his student accommodation, spend time in the sunshine, study and save money.

Many online students who study at a distance do something similar. They go off to a part of the world they enjoy or want to visit and hook up their laptop wherever they are. Some students study while constantly travelling. The travel blogger, Megan Jerrard, has pictures on her blog of her completing a thesis in a tent in the Australian outback, doing research in Costa Rica, and writing an assignment at the side of a swimming pool in Florida. Meanwhile, Projects Abroad has launched "Backpack University". Projects Abroad is the world's largest organisation that arranges international volunteering and internships, amongst other activities. "Backpack University" combines a variety of travel options with studying online at the same time.

For most students, though, the decision will be about which room in the family home to use as their study. For others, they might want to leave their parents and set up a shared house with their mates, so they can recreate the social experience they might have had by studying at a traditional university. Some students, of course, will be in student accommodation at a traditional university because they will be doing "hybrid" learning with some online and some face-to-face, such as being in a flipped classroom. Ultimately, it means there are plenty of choices as to where to study.

> QUICK TIP: Think carefully about the places you can study and choose a "top three" which you might alternate depending on the circumstances.

There are two factors when selecting a place to study which are worthy of considering. The first is just how much privacy you can get. Studying requires thinking, and most people need somewhere quiet where they will not be uninterrupted if they want to think deeply. If you are an 18-year-old about to start university studies for the first time, you might find it challenging if you have younger siblings in the house. University study involves more thinking and analysis than you have ever done in high school or at A-level. Indeed, many new university students are somewhat surprised at the amount of time they are left on their own by their lecturers, just to think. If you found it tough with siblings at home when doing A-levels, you may well find university study even harder in such a situation. Indeed, when I spoke with students about the sudden change from campus study to online learning during the Coronavirus pandemic, they often complained about siblings. "They just don't understand what we have to go through", said one student to me. "I love them to bits, but they are really annoying when I am trying to study".

The second factor to consider about the location for your studying is how social you can be. Students learn from each other. They swap ideas and exchange information of all kinds. Being alone at home will reduce your ability to benefit from the social aspect of study. After high school, you may be one of only a couple of your friends who have stayed at home. The rest may have gone off to a campus university or taken a "gap year" travelling. If several remain at home, learning at a distance, then you can carry on meeting them socially. However, you might not wish to be isolated. Hence, setting up a shared house could be an advantage, apart from the apparent cost issue. Even so, it is worthwhile thinking about the social side of studying at a distance. You will benefit from chatting with other students – even if they are doing different courses.

If you are going to a traditional university but will be doing some form of hybrid learning, then you will not need to worry about the considerations as to where to study. That will have been decided for you by the university. It's only if you are staying at home, or studying at a distance, you should really think carefully about where you should study. Ultimately, you need a place where you can concentrate and think, free of interruptions. It might be time to ask your parents for one of those "garden rooms" where you can be alone away from the rest of the family during study times ...! Indeed, one student would have probably preferred such a possibility having told me,

> *Studying online at home means that your bedroom or living room now becomes your place of learning. This means it is harder to relax and not think about studying and all the work you could do even late at night. It makes you feel guilty for not studying when you're trying to relax.*

▶ NEGOTIATE WITH YOUR HOUSEHOLD

If you are studying at home, you need to set some ground rules. Traditional university students either in university accommodation or in a shared house, don't have to worry about rules relating to studying. Everyone is in the same situation and understands what people mean by saying, "I need some space now to study". It is a shared experience, so students living together rarely need to negotiate things like study time or quiet time. That doesn't mean they don't have to have rules about who cleans the fridge, or when the bins are emptied ...! However, everything to do with studying is common ground among a group of students.

That's not the same for students who are at home, studying at a distance. When they want to study, another household member probably wants to do something else that could create noise or distraction. Parents want to have their friends around for dinner, or siblings want to get their mates around to listen to music or play games in the garden. Studying at university level is challenging – indeed, if it were easy, there would be no value in having a degree. Other members of the household need to understand that your study time is valuable and that you need to be able to concentrate. If you don't establish how everyone in the household should deal with your valuable study time, conflict is inevitable. You want to study, and the rest of the household wants to party. According to Jane Gunn, a professional mediator and conflict management consultant, preparing in advance for inevitable conflict means it is much easier to handle when it arises. She says, "Having an agreed system or plan for handling conflicts can help us to manage them more easily at a much earlier stage, and so avoid the problems and costs of escalation" (Gunn, 2010). It is, therefore, a good idea to explain to the rest of the family the importance of your study time and what you expect from them to help you. However, if you agree on a way to resolve any disputes when they arise (and they will happen), you will find it easier to deal with them. Another important aspect of negotiating these rules is the principle of "reciprocity". According to the negotiation expert Derek Arden, reciprocity is when you help others get what they want so that they will, in return, help you get what you want. In his book, *Win-Win*, Derek explains that people who try to help others in any negotiation get better results (Arden, 2015). This means that when you set out the ground rules you expect from the rest of the household, you will be more likely to get them to agree if you set out what you will also do for them. For example, you could say that once a week, you'll head off to the local library for the day, leaving everyone else to do what they want without having to worry about disturbing you.

> **QUICK TIP: Never delay negotiating or discussing your study needs. If you do, it will lead to bigger problems in the future.**

▶ THE PROBLEMS OF SHARING TECHNOLOGY

The main requirement for studying online is a reliable Internet connection. However, everyone else in the house also wants to use the same connection. They want to watch Netflix, play on the Xbox, or do the shopping. It means that even with high-speed broadband connections, there can be competition from the rest of the family for enough bandwidth. Online studying involves a great deal of video. There are many recorded lectures to watch, and you will need to take part in several live video conferences. That means you will need a good slice of the available bandwidth. If you have relatively limited broadband in the house, you could find your studies interrupted. Videos will lag or pixelate when other household members are watching streaming TV or playing online games. But they will also have difficulties if you are using a great deal of bandwidth for studies. It is a recipe for arguments ...!

There are two ways out of the problems caused by having to share broadband bandwidth. One is to upgrade the broadband account, so you have greater bandwidth. If you can get "fibre to the home" (FTTH) or "fibre to the premises" (FTTP) broadband, this will be ideal. Many fibre broadband suppliers only operate "fibre to the cabinet" (FTTC) broadband. This only provides fibre speeds to the telecoms boxes in the street. The remainder of the journey to your home uses copper cables, which are slower than fibre. As a result, you can't get the top speeds. You can get very high speeds, but it depends on the distance between your home and the telecoms cabinet. However, the supply of the top speed FTTP is limited. Only a few operators supply this form of broadband, and it is more expensive. Even so, it is worthwhile investigating if you can get better broadband in your area. Even if you can only get FTTH broadband, some suppliers use technology to squeeze more speed out of the system.

If you cannot get better broadband in your area or can't afford it, you will need to consider the second way out of the problem of sharing the connection with others in the household. This is about scheduling and cooperating. You might need to consider watching your online lecture videos in the mornings, leaving the family to be able to stream TV in the evenings, for example. Carefully timetabling your study periods to fit in with the rest of the house can save arguments and make studying a more enjoyable experience as you won't suffer lags on video lectures. Also, check out your broadband router's settings. On some, you can change the priorities of devices during certain hours. That means you could give greater priority to your laptop during study hours and to the TV or games device at other times. Ultimately, though, if you have to share your broadband with others in the house, you will have to negotiate who gets priority and when.

For some students, this will not be the only issue of shared technology. Not every family can afford a computer for each member of the household. That means you may only have access to one family computer for your studies. With other people at home needing to use the same machine, there will need to be a plan as to who uses the computer and when. Thinking about this before you start your studies will save annoyance and argument at a later date.

▶ SETTING UP YOUR STUDY ROOM

Ideally, when you are studying at a distance, you will have a dedicated room in which you can concentrate on your studies. Often, this will be your bedroom. But sometimes, there is not enough space and so you may need to study in the kitchen, or the dining room if you have one. Wherever you are going to study, it is worthwhile taking some time to consider the best set-up before you begin your studies. Getting the room right at the outset will make studying more manageable and more enjoyable.

Choosing a desk

If you don't already have a desk, make sure you get a good appropriate one before starting your studies. A desk will be better than a kitchen or dining table as it will be at a more appropriate height. Typically you will only sit at a kitchen or dining table for a short amount of time. However, you can be studying for several hours, so the desk needs to be at a height that allows you to work comfortably for long periods. So, getting a proper desk is going to be helpful to you as you study for your degree over several years.

It would be a good idea to buy the most expensive desk you can afford. Cheap desks will probably not last long. Besides, one of the reasons why they cost less is because they are smaller than standard desks. A typical office desk is 120cm wide and 80cm deep. Many cheap "home computer" desks are smaller than this. The result will be that you do not have enough space, and working under cramped conditions will not make for easy study.

Ideally, you would have a "sit-stand" desk. This is an adjustable desk that raises and lowers. This means that you can sometimes sit down to do some work, and at other times you can stand up. Sitting down for hours on end is not good for your health. Several studies have shown that occasionally standing throughout the day can be beneficial to overall health. Indeed, research shows that people who use "sit-stand" desks have better cardiovascular health and have other improved physiological markers (Carr et al., 2016, and Bodker et al., 2021). However, there are other benefits to sit-stand desks besides avoiding the health damage of remaining too sedentary. Research in Texas has demonstrated that workers who use sit-stand desks increase their productivity by more than 50 per cent (Garrett et al., 2016). For students, this is important. Sit-stand desks appear to make you more efficient. This means they can be helpful when you are under pressure for assignments, for instance. There is more about sit-stand desks in Chapter 11.

Select a good chair

Students on campus will be sitting at their desks on chairs provided by the university. You will be amazed at the cost of such chairs. Even though the university will have bought chairs in the most cost-effective way, they also have a responsibility to people on their premises in terms of health and safety. As a result, the chairs provided for working at desks will have several ergonomic features to help ensure comfort. Buying a cheap chair is counterproductive. You will end up having to buy several chairs over the three or four years of a degree. The chair will get a great deal of use, so it needs to be comfortable and reliable. In much the same way as the desk, opt for the most expensive chair you can afford.

According to the Consumers' Association, it is essential to get a comfortable chair that can prevent muscle strain (Morgan, 2021). Whether you select a grand leather chair, one made of mesh, or a chair that allows you to kneel on it is more of a personal choice. What is essential for students who are studying online is that they consider health and safety in much the same way as a campus university would do for students on their premises. Investing in a good chair will help ensure your studying is comfortable and helps your overall well-being. There are plenty of websites that provide advice on choosing a good chair. Ultimately, that advice comes down to having a chair that is adjustable, and that has good back support.

Where will you sit?

The position of your desk and chair in the room is essential. You will want to sit in a situation where your desk and computer screen are not subject to shadows or reflections. As you will see in Chapter 11, one of the main difficulties with studying online is its impact on your eyes. Throughout an online degree, you will be looking at a computer for several years, which means it is crucial to take steps to help ensure your eyes are not affected. Part of that process is thinking about where the desk will be.

If your desk has a window behind it, your screen will have annoying reflections that cause you to strain your eyes or miss important details in what you are viewing. Equally, if you sit with a window behind you, the video conference calls you take part in will not be good because you will be in silhouette. Furthermore, according to the Feng Shui master, Sarah McAllister, the best position for your desk is diagonally opposite the door, facing into the room (McAllister, 2020). If you have a wall behind you, then you will feel protected.

If you sit facing a window so that the light does not reflect on your screen and you become visible on video conference calls, there is the danger that you will be distracted by what is going on outside your room. Plus, you are likely to have the door behind you in this arrangement, which means you could be constantly worried about potential interruptions.

Obviously, there will be practical considerations as to where you can put your desk. However, many people just put the desk against the wall without thinking what that would mean for studying over the long term. Getting the position of the desk right at the outset will help you ensure that your studies are less prone to problems and difficulties. Ergonomics experts suggest that if you cannot get the ideal position for your desk, having the window to the side is a good compromise. This means you will have natural light falling on your desk, but you will be less distracted and avoid the issue of reflections on the screen.

Lighting the room

You are going to be reading and watching a great deal of material online. However, you will also be using paper documents and books, as well as making your own handwritten notes. This means you need to think carefully about lighting in your study room. You will need lighting that doesn't reflect on the screen and allows you to see the type clearly when looking at print. When students only studied using printed materials, a single desk lamp was all that was needed. However, when studying online, you will be switching from computer screen to print, to mobile phone and back again. If these are not illuminated well, you could suffer eyestrain and be less productive as you have to keep arranging things so you can see them clearly. As a result, spending time and money on setting up the lighting is worthwhile for the long term. Indeed, according to the lighting expert Mike Cheong, there is a relationship between good lighting and grades achieved when studying. In other words, getting the lighting right could help you gain a better degree (Cheong, 2020). When looking for suitable lights, check the "lighting temperature", which is a number such as "6500K". According to Mike Cheong, the best colour temperature for studying is from 4000K to 6500K. He adds,

> *A longer LED lamp with bulbs will disperse the light more evenly across a bigger area. A small spotlight will keep the light in one specific area, meaning you might have to move your book or equipment to read and study.*

QUICK TIP: Try to avoid buying cheap lighting. You will be studying a great deal of your time indoors facing a computer screen. Get the best lighting you can afford and you will avoid several problems caused by poor lights.

▶ CHOOSING THE RIGHT HARDWARE

With your room set up to allow you to work well, your next consideration will be the technology you need. You might think, "all I need is a laptop", and, in one sense, that is all you need for online study. However, there are many other aspects to studying online where the choice of technology becomes an important factor. If you don't get the right technology at the outset, it can lead to frustration, annoyance, and reduced productivity later on. Hence, getting your technology choices right from the start will save time and money.

Laptop or desktop?

You will need a computer to study online, and it might seem a good idea to get a laptop. If you want to study in the library or a coffee shop, rather than at home, having a laptop will be essential. Equally, if you are studying in a hybrid way, with some face-to-face teaching and some online, you will need a laptop for those in-person sessions. However, laptops have limitations that can make studying online more cumbersome and awkward. Plus, they tend to be slower than desktop computers, which means that those fractions of seconds over the years of study could add up to many hours of lost time. However, the British online technology magazine, *TechRadar*, suggests that deciding between a laptop and desktop is not straightforward because each kind of device has several advantages (Key, 2021). One factor, though, may be costs. *TechRadar* says that getting a laptop with the same specification as a desktop will cost more money. So, if you want the best specification, a desktop works out more cost-effective.

Ultimately, you will have to compromise – or buy two machines, a desktop and a laptop. That will give you the best of both items of technology, though it will obviously double your costs. Table 2.1 compares desktops and laptops to help you consider what will work best in your specific circumstance.

If you have selected a laptop, you should also invest in a laptop "riser". This is a device that raises the laptop above the desk's surface

TABLE 2.1 Desktop or laptop?

Desktop	Laptop
Cheaper than similar powered laptops	High specification machines cost more
Can use any size screen	Limited screen size
Expandable as your studies grow	Difficult to expand if you run out of space
Easy to add peripherals, such as cameras	Cameras and microphones relatively poor
Difficult to damage	Can be dropped or easily broken
Well-secured in a locked home	Easily stolen when out and about
Not flexible if your study patterns change	Can adapt to changing ways of study
Only used in one location	Can be used anywhere

and allows you to angle the screen so that it is level with your eyes. Otherwise, you could suffer from neck pain and headaches if you are hunched over a laptop on your desk for many hours.

> QUICK TIP: *If you can't afford a sit-stand desk, look online for portable risers that can move your screen and keyboard up and down on a standard desk.*

Keyboards and mice

Whichever computer hardware you buy for your studies, you will need some additional peripheral devices. If you are using a desktop, you will need a mouse and keyboard. However, you will also benefit from these if you have a laptop. That's because the keyboard and trackpad on a laptop are small and can lead to muscle fatigue when you use them for a long time. Studying online will lead to many hours of use of the keyboard and mouse. Hence, even if you have a laptop with its own integrated keyboard, adding an external device for when you are working at home is a good idea. It will help save you from muscular issues associated with using narrow keyboards and trackpads. Also, make sure you invest in a good keyboard or mouse that is comfortable to use. Many desktop computers are provided with a keyboard and mouse, but these tend to be cheap affairs. Far better to find a keyboard and mouse that are comfortable to use and fit your way of working. You will be using these devices for a long time, and if you don't get good ones at the outset, you will waste money by having to buy new ones in the future. At the same time, you could make your studying less comfortable and have muscular aches and pains, all of which will have an impact on your work.

> QUICK TIP: *Even if you have a laptop, get an external mouse device. It will save you time and help reduce muscle strain.*

Get some headphones

When studying online, you will be spending a great deal of your time listening to recorded lectures and other audio materials. If you are studying in the family home, the noise this creates could be annoying to the rest of the household. Equally, their noise could disturb your concentration when trying to listen to a lecture. A set of noise-cancelling headphones or earbuds can help you concentrate and prevent arguments with the family. Research has shown that when you are in a relatively noisy environment, your performance at completing tasks increases when you wear noise-cancelling headphones (Molesworth et al., 2013).

Buy a top-notch webcam

Webcams are an essential component of studying online. However, these devices are highly variable in terms of performance and capabilities. As with so many other items of technology, the more you pay, the better the device. So, get the most expensive webcam you can afford. In Chapter 6, you will find out more about using webcams to their best effect. However, when considering your preparation for online study, you need to think about which webcam you will get. It needs to last and perform well because you will inevitably be involved in many online video calls. Trying to save money by getting a cheap webcam will reduce your enjoyment of your online studies and may hinder your performance in online classes.

Consider an extra microphone

One of the main problems with online video is the poor sound quality. According to Dr Jonas Köster from Stanford University, sound quality can have a negative impact on online video overall (Köster, 2018). Although he was talking about the production of video recordings, it is important to realise that as a student you will be part of "videos". These will include video conference calls, such as Zoom or Microsoft Teams. However, you may also be required to participate in group presentations that are recorded online and form part of your assessment. If you can't be heard clearly, then this could affect your marks. As with a camera, get the best microphone you can afford. An external microphone that plugs into a USB port on your computer is the best solution as it means you can use the microphone with a desktop or laptop.

Get a printer

Studying online involves a great deal of reading web pages, online documents, and ebooks, so you might not think you need a printer. Think again ...! Even though you are entering a digital world of learning, you will find that printed information is handy. Indeed, you may even find that you will gain better marks by printing out the online reading materials and reading hard copy. According to Professor Naomi Baron, from Stanford University, it can be more challenging to concentrate when reading online. Plus, it is easier to get distracted while using the digital world (Baron, 2021). As a result, printing out material that you really need to focus on or which requires concentration will help you. In addition, you can highlight things when they are printed out or scribble notes on the pages. Also, there will be times in your studies when you have to print things out. For instance, you may be involved in projects or work for your dissertation where you have to show participants a printed privacy notice. If you can't print things out yourself, you will find this awkward and time-consuming. Luckily, suitable printers are relatively low cost these days – it is the ink that is more expensive. So, consider getting an ink subscription. The leading printer manufacturers offer these, and you can save money as well as be sure that you never run out of ink.

> **QUICK TIP:** If you want to use a highlighter to mark up printed documents make sure you get one that is "printer friendly". Otherwise the highlighting could inadvertently remove the text you are marking up.

▶ SELECTING THE RIGHT SOFTWARE

There will be little choice for many students in terms of the software you will use for your studies. This is because the university will have an online teaching, learning, and assessment system that will require all students to use the software provided. In many instances, this will be an office suite, such as Microsoft Office 365. Before you begin your online studies, it is a good idea to find out from your university if they are going to provide you with a subscription to an office programme. This will avoid you needing to buy the software yourself. Also, by asking in advance of your studies, it will allow you to familiarise yourself with the software you have to use, as you should be able to get a trial version before you begin studying. If your university does not provide you with office software, such as a word processor, then make sure you check out the student discounts available. Many software publishers provide education discounts, but you may have to hunt for them on their websites. Also, organisations like UNiDAYS and Student Beans provide access to discounted software, so they are also worth checking out.

Another piece of software that you will have no choice but to use will be the Virtual Learning Environment or VLE. This is like the "central station" for your online studies, where you will find each of the modules, your assignments, study resources, and general university information. There are several standard VLE packages available, and your university will use one such as Moodle, Blackboard, or Canvas. Before your studies begin, find out which system is used by your university. You will then be able to watch some introductory videos about the software on YouTube. That way, you will familiarise yourself with the program before your studies begin, giving you a head start. It is worthwhile getting to know the VLE software. Every year I have students who have not bothered to get to grips with it. Then, they call me in a panic as they cannot find something, or at the last minute realise they don't know how to submit their assignment. Getting to know the VLE in advance will help you avoid such stressful situations.

QUICK TIP: There are plenty of videos on YouTube that demonstrate the various VLE systems, so you can familiarise yourself with the software before you start your studies.

Choose a good web browser

Your computer may already have a web browser installed when you buy it. However, the pre-installed web browser may not be the most appropriate one for you. Besides, it may not be entirely compatible with your university systems. Also, if you accept the standard browser, or the one you were told to use at school, it suggests you are not ready to take the initiative – and that is an essential requirement for a university student. In his book *Originals*, Professor Adam Grant, an organisational psychologist, points out that when people choose their own browser, they remain in their jobs 15 per cent longer than those who stick with the status quo (Grant, 2016). The people who chose their own browser were also 19 per cent more likely to avoid skipping work. The research that discovered this showed that it was nothing to do with technical skills but was about being able to take the initiative. If you stick with the pre-set browser on your computer or use the one you have always had because it's the one Mum and Dad suggested, you run the risk of not doing as well as you could by taking the initiative. Besides, quite apart from the most popular web browsers, there are others targeted at students, which include integrated notetaking, for example.

Get a backup program

Whenever I set a module assignment, I am confident I will get a call from a student on the submission date saying they have suffered some kind of computer glitch and cannot send me their work. It happens every time, and I am no longer surprised. It seems as though students haven't realised that their digital work is fragile and can disappear. You can, for example, hit the delete key by mistake. Or you could forget to press the "Save" button. There could even be a technical glitch with your computer meaning it rendered your files unreadable. These issues can be minimised if you have backups of everything you do. Too many students try to rely on manual backups, such as copying their work to a memory stick. But that also has problems. What if you forget to do it or drop the memory stick down the toilet? Yes, students have told me they've done that. The answer is to automate your backups. There is a wide variety of good backup software around, so check out the student discounts available. Plus, do not rely on saying it is "in the cloud". If you delete a file on your computer by mistake, then the syncing software could delete it from the cloud storage service as well. All too often, people think they have a backup when they don't. Ideally, you should have three copies of everything you do – the original, the cloud version, and a physical backup on a separate hard drive. Backup software will manage those versions for you, and therefore if something does go wrong, you can be sure you will have at least one file to go back to.

Other useful programs

There are many other potentially useful software programs that you could investigate before you start your studies. However, at the early stage of your studies, it is worthwhile considering programs that will help you with:

- To-do lists
- Calendars and schedules
- Tracking your work.

Crucial to your success as an online student will be keeping up with the work and sticking to the timetable. Selecting the software that can help you achieve this before you begin your studies is a good idea. That way, you can practise using it first, and you can be ready to get on with studying without falling behind. There are plenty of "to-do" list programs and apps available, so it is worthwhile taking time to find the one that works best for you and the way you work. There are also programs that will enable you to plan and schedule work more efficiently. These include Trello, Airtable, and Clickup.

PRACTICAL TIPS

- **Choose a primary study location.** Organise a place to study which will be your base for your online work. You don't always have to work from there, but it will be your primary study location. If you have a central base for studying, your brain will subconsciously associate the location with studies.
- **Agree with others on your priorities.** Unless you live alone, you will need to negotiate with the rest of the household about your quiet times and the need to share broadband connections.
- **Plan your room.** Make sure you set up the room so that it works for studying. Online studies mean you will be on your own in front of a computer for long periods of time. So setting up the room properly at the outset will reap the rewards later.
- **Sort out the technology in advance.** For anyone studying online, there is a dependence upon technology. So make sure you have the proper hardware and software in place and that you have organised things like backups and scheduling software before you start studying.

▶ REFERENCES

Anon (n.d.) 'Backpack University|Projects Abroad', Projects Abroad. Available at: www.projects-abroad.co.uk/study-abroad/backpack-university (Accessed: 23 August 2021).

Arden, D. (2015) *Win-Win*, London, Pearson.

Baron, N.S. (2021) *How We Read Now*. Oxford: Oxford University Press.

Bodker, A., Visotcky, A., Gutterman, D., Widlansky, M.E. and Kulinski, J. (2021) 'The Impact of Standing Desks on Cardiometabolic and Vascular Health', *Vascular Medicine*, 26(4), pp. 374–382.

Carr, L.J., Swift, M., Ferrer, A. and Benzo, R. (2016) 'Cross-Sectional Examination of Long-Term Access to Sit–Stand Desks in a Professional Office Setting', *American Journal of Preventive Medicine*, 50(1), pp. 96–100.

Cheong, M. (2020) 'The Best Lighting for Studying and Reading', TaoTronics Blog. Available at: https://blog.taotronics.com/home-garden/light ing/the-best-lighting-for-studying-and-reading (Accessed: 29 August 2021).

Garrett, G., Benden, M., Mehta, R., Pickens, A., Peres, S.C. and Zhao, H. (2016) 'Call Center Productivity over 6 Months Following a Standing Desk Intervention', *IIE Transactions on Occupational Ergonomics and Human Factors*, 4(2–3), pp. 188–195.

Grant, A. (2016) *Originals*. London: Penguin Random House.

Gunn, J. (2010) *How to Beat Bedlam in the Boardroom and Boredom in the Bedroom*'. Evesham: HotHive Books.

Jerrard, M. (2014) 'The Best Way to Juggle International Travel While Studying Full Time', Mapping Megan. Available at: www.mappingme gan.com/juggle-international-travel-study-full-time (Accessed: 23 August 2021).

Key, K. (2021) 'Laptop vs Desktop: Which Should You Buy?', TechRadar. Available at: www.techradar.com/uk/news/laptop-vs-desktop-which-should-you-buy (Accessed: 29 August 2021).

Köster, J. (2018) *Video in the Age of Digital Learning*. Cham: Springer.

McAllister, S. (2020) 'Home Office Feng Shui'. Available at: www.feng shuiagency.com/home-office-feng-shui (Accessed: 29 August 2021).

Molesworth, B.R.C., Burgess, M. and Kwon, D. (2013) 'The Use of Noise Cancelling Headphones to Improve Concurrent Task Performance in a Noisy Environment', *Applied Acoustics*, 74(1), pp. 110–115.

Morgan, T. (2021) 'Choosing the Best Home Office Chair', *Which?* Available at: www.which.co.uk/reviews/working-from-home/article/home-office-guides/choosing-the-best-home-office-chair-a3xNL3D4SFUJ (Accessed: 28 August 2021).

Popov, A.V. (2018) 'Historical Development Stages of the Student Youth Accommodation Architecture from Dormitories Prototypes to Post-Industrial University Campuses', *International Journal of Civil Engineering and Technology*, 9(11), pp. 2526–2536.

Part II

Studying online

3 Reading online

It doesn't matter whether you are studying on campus or in your bedroom at a distance; you will be doing a great deal of reading. Every module for a degree course is calculated in "credit units". There are 360 credit units for a degree in the UK. Most other countries have similar concepts, though the calculation of credit units may be different. Each unit is equivalent to one hour of work each week. Hence a typical 20 unit module is 20 hours of study. Of that, around four hours will be "contact time" – that's lectures and seminars with academic staff. So that leaves 16 hours each week for a 20 unit module in which you have to study yourself. Some of that time will be researching, thinking, making notes, and going back over the information to consolidate what you have been learning. That is reckoned to be about half of the hours you have to yourself. That means, on a 20 unit module, you are left with eight hours which is reading time. Typically, you are expected to do two hours of reading for every hour of lectures or seminars. Sometimes this will be "guided reading", where your lecturer will have set specific chapters to read. However, you will also be expected to do some "self-directed" reading, where you find relevant material independently, without any guidance from the lecturer. Some modules will have more guided reading than self-directed

DOI: 10.4324/9781003259695-5

reading, but other modules might be entirely dependent upon you finding material to read. Either way, there is a lot of reading to do. Over the course of a year for a degree, you will do 120 credit units. Generally, you can expect to be studying three modules simultaneously, though it will depend upon the credits applied to each individual module. Typically, with three simultaneous 20 credit modules, each having around eight hours of reading a week, it means you will be expected to do a total of 24 hours of reading each week. If you are not careful, you will get "boggle-eyed" and exhausted.

▶ HOW WE READ

Getting to know how we read can help you study better. That's because you will be able to take into account what your brain and body are doing when you read. You can then adapt to ensure you don't overexert yourself with the vast amount of reading that a university degree requires. When you learned to read, you were taught how to read and what to do so that you could understand the material. But when we are at junior school learning how to read, we are not taught anything about what our brain or body is doing. It means we only really know half the story about reading. Many people get tired when reading, they find it difficult to concentrate, and they get bored quickly. That's because they are not accommodating to deal with the body's reaction to reading. Understanding how we read can help alleviate many of the problems associated with reading. Remember, in a typical study week, you will spend around half of each day just reading. It is the most important activity for any degree student, so it is worthwhile spending some time trying to understand what you will be doing.

You are not a "smooth eyes"

If you have ever watched someone reading, you will have been surprised that their eyes do not go smoothly across the page. Instead, as they move from left to right over the text, their eyes repeatedly jump up and down. You might not be able to see how many times their eyes jerk around because each movement lasts for only about 20 milliseconds. These jerky jumps are called *saccades*, which is the French word for "jerks" and describes the movements very well indeed. Between these bursts of energy, the eyes settle on the text in what is known as a "fixation". Ultimately, when we read, what we are doing is taking a series of individual "snapshots" as we jump along the text (Crowder and Wagner, 1992). Your eyes are doing a great deal of muscular activity when you read, which is partly why you can get tired quickly. This is an issue when studying, as you will need to read a great deal of material. The fact that your eyeballs will be doing plenty of bouncing around means that you have the potential for eye strain unless you take care.

> **QUICK TIP:** Pay close attention to the way you read online, as it can cause eyestrain and headaches if you do not have a plan for coping with digital reading.

You listen as you read

As you are reading this text, you can probably "hear" the words. Of course, you are not actually hearing the words unless you have the audiobook version. However, your brain doesn't just process the text in the visual region at the back of your head. It also passes the text through something known as the "phonological loop". That's a fancy way of saying you are checking the sounds the words make. It means that if you come across a word you have never seen before, you can probably make sense of it from the sounds. However, this means your brain is now doing two activities at the same time. It is visually analysing the text and checking what it sounds like. As a result, your brain is using energy, and the depletion of your reserves can contribute to feeling tired. When you have been reading for a while, you will probably feel tired. That's because your brain has done double the work. For some people, there is a third activity that contributes to helping you read and adds to the energy used. These people "subvocalise". They are almost reading out loud, but not quite. Sometimes you can see their lips move as they read. Research at the University of Massachusetts established over 40 years ago that subvocalisation can improve comprehension (Slowiaczek and Clifton, 1980). Indeed, educationalists suggested this technique back in the 1940s to help children read better (Buswell, 1947). However, even though it helps children learn to read, it adds to the effort of reading. Is it any wonder that you get tired reading with the visual centre of your brain working on the text, your phonological loop activated, and sometimes subvocalising the text? That is a lot of cognitive activity which can make you tired. For online studying, though, there is the additional complication of reading on screen.

▶ ON-SCREEN READING IS EXTRA TIRING

Reading from a screen is not the same as reading from a printed page. Several differences impact how well you can read the text and how much you comprehend or remember. When you are reading from a printed book or document, the light reaching your eyes is scattered. There are several beams of light reflecting from the page in various directions. Your eyes are getting this reflected light which is how you usually see things. However, screens project light directly into your eyeballs. The light is not scattered but is effectively injected into your eyes. That is not how your eyes were designed to receive light. Didn't your Mum tell you not to look directly at the sun? To cope with the light that is flooding into your eyes, they have to work harder than they would if you were reading from a printed book. As you will discover in Chapter 11, this can lead to something called Computer Vision Syndrome, a clinical diagnosis for people suffering problems resulting from sitting at screens for long periods. Reading online is tiring and can cause health problems. We also appear to make it even more difficult for ourselves because the way we read online differs from how we read printed materials. Rather than reading the text logically, we take a more scattered approach when we read online. We tend to scan the page, looking at various different items before we return to the top to read the text. Much research has been conducted using eye tracking technology. This is where people are asked to read online material and special equipment detects how their eyes move. These movements can then be mapped onto specific parts of the web page so that the researchers can detect what is being read by the web page visitors. Many studies have been undertaken using this research technique. There is widespread confirmation that people do not read online logically. Instead, people's eyes roam around the page, apparently looking for something familiar (Pernice, Whitenton, and Nielsen, 2014).

> **QUICK TIP:** *If you find it hard to read online, consider printing out the essential pages you need to concentrate on.*

Furthermore, much of the printed material we use has been given careful consideration regarding typography. There are well-established protocols for printed material for the number of characters and words on a line, for instance. However, much of what we read online is not prepared by graphic designers with typographical experience. As a result, fonts are often selected without much regard for their readability. For example, even a tiny change in type size can significantly alter our reading speed online (Bernard, Liao, and Mills, 2001). In addition, the width of the lines of text is often not well-controlled. This means the number of characters on a line is widely variable and often beyond what is comfortable for the eyes to take in. That means it is harder to read online text, and it involves many more reading errors, taking more time than the equivalent printed material. This is another reason why reading digital materials can be very tiring indeed.

As if the process of reading were not tricky enough online, there is the additional problem of how we use computers. We tend to

remain relatively static and fixed in position when we use computers. That's not the same as when we sit and read a printed book.
When we read a book, we adjust our position more frequently,
plus we look away from the book at regular intervals. When we

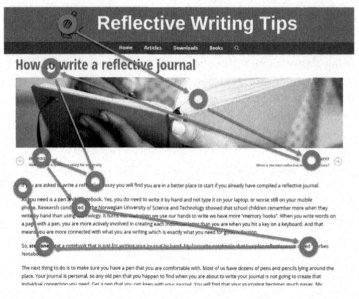

Figure 3.1 How a reader's eyes move around a page

TABLE 3.1 Differences between reading in print and online

Reading in print	Reading online
Relies on scattered reflective light (normal vision)	Relies on projected direct injection of transmitted light (not normal vision)
We tend to move our body around when reading	We tend to remain relatively fixed in one position
Uses well-established typography making it easy on the eye	Typography can be variable and not helpful to the eye

read online, we stare at the screen in a rather rigid position. This tenses our muscles which, in turn, leads to tiredness. Our eyes, in particular, get tired by constantly staring at the screen.

PACE YOUR ONLINE READING

As you have seen, online reading is tiring and challenging. It can impact your health too. Many students tend to do a great deal of online reading around assignment time or in the revision period in the run-up to exams. This is not a good idea. Quite apart from the impact on your sight and general well-being, long periods of reading online will affect your cognitive capabilities. That means that you will find it harder to concentrate and remember what you are reading due to being tired. For people accessing digital textbooks and other online reading materials, it is even more critical that they manage their time for reading. People who read traditional paper-based documents will get tired and find it hard to concentrate after long periods of reading. However, when you read online, these difficulties can arise sooner. Even if you have always planned your reading activities when studying, you need to consider an even more detailed plan for when you read online.

For example, it might take you a couple of hours to go through a chapter of an academic textbook. Students get used to the rhythm of reading and can look at a textbook and think, "that's going to take an hour" or "that chapter is a two-hour read". Of course, you might not be consciously thinking this, but you get an idea in your head about how much time a particular piece of reading will take, based on your previous experience. You might, for instance, schedule an evening to go through the relevant chapter in the book and make your notes.

However, if you were to do the same for the online textbook, there is a good chance you will not get the scheduling right. Research conducted in the USA showed that people are more aware of their performance when reading on paper than they are when reading online (Clinton, 2019). The study also found that reading performance suffers when we read online. So, if you have scheduled your time for online reading based upon your experience of reading in print, you are not likely to get the same benefit from the material. Essentially, you need more time to read online materials than the comparable items in print.

Combine the additional time needed to read online, together with the tiring effect of reading digital documents, and it is clear you need a completely different approach to planning your reading activities. If we consider the typical two-hour reading of a printed book chapter, ideally, you need to think about doubling that for dealing with the same material in digital form. Plus, given the ease with which you will become tired and lack concentration, it means that the overall time taken needs to be broken down into much shorter reading sessions. This will help prevent tiredness and improve concentration. Ideally, you should read online for no more than 15–20 minutes at a time and take a rest between each of those sessions for at least five to ten minutes. Several studies have shown that taking a break between cognitive activities can improve recall and comprehension. Indeed, in one research study undertaken at the University of Edinburgh, neuroscientists discovered that if people took a ten-minute break after reading, they were better able to remember what they had read a week later compared with people who didn't take a break (Dewar et al., 2012). Importantly, it was the kind of break that was taken that was important. It needed to be a restful break where you just do nothing. It looks like these breaks are essential to let your subconscious process what you have just been reading.

> *QUICK TIP: Read online materials in sections of 15–20 minutes followed by a five- to ten-minute break.*

▶ READ WITH MUSIC IN THE BACKGROUND

Music can enhance your learning. Several studies show how music improves performance. Professional athletes are well known for having an inspirational playlist that they listen to while training to spur them on. It works. Many amateur athletes and those who run for fitness will also have experienced the benefits of listening to music while training. Academic reading is really training for your brain. So it makes sense to consider whether background music can improve your reading. Research in Germany, for instance, found that for people who already have good memory skills, background music helped improve their comprehension of what they were reading (Lehmann and Seufert, 2017). However, in people with a lower memory capacity, background music did not help. Indeed it decreased the ability of such students to recall what they had read. The research, though, used instrumental versions of familiar tracks. So, the participants may have mentally inserted the lyrics while trying to read and thereby hampered their performance. This is also suggested with another study on music and a task requiring attention when reading random letters. The American researchers found that performance deteriorated when music with lyrics was played (Oliver, Levy, and Baldwin, 2021). These two studies taken together imply that instrumental background music that is not associated with any lyrics could help your reading performance; hence it is worth a try.

There is another reason why you may wish to read with some background music. If you listen to background music, especially through noise-cancelling headphones, you may find concentration improves. This is because other background noises, especially people talking, can distract you and reduce your concentration. Chinese researchers found that background noise and irrelevant speech can impair your ability to read (Yan et al., 2018). When you are studying online, you are likely to be at home with other people in the household. If they are busy chatting in the background, or you can hear noises as they watch TV in another room, your ability to read effectively is likely to fall. Listening to instrumental music through noise-cancelling headphones could cut out the irrelevant noises and help you to concentrate, as well as improve your comprehension of what you are reading. There is more detail about using background music to avoid distractions in Chapter 10.

▶ PRINT OUT LONG ITEMS OF READING

As suggested in Chapter 2, a printer can be handy for you when studying online and at a distance. At a traditional campus-based university, you would be able to pop into the library to get printed books if that is what you prefer to read. Plus, university libraries have banks of printers and copiers available so that you can print things out quickly. When you are at home, studying alone, you don't have easy access to such facilities. However, the library and its facilities are an essential aspect of university life. Indeed, on most campuses, you will find the main library is centrally located, with more specialist libraries available within each of the schools or faculties of the university. Whatever you might think about the value of digital documents, students love printed items. Every year in one of the modules that I teach about the digital economy, I get students to complete a poll about the books they are reading. I've been doing this for the past 15 years. Each time I run the little survey, I ask students whether they prefer to read ebooks or printed books. The results have been consistent and have shown no sign of changing. Nearly 90 per cent of students prefer printed books to digital ones. Almost all the students who prefer digital books have been those who have another first language, as English is their second or third language. For them the digital books are better as they can more easily get portions of text translated online to help with their understanding. For students with English as their first language, printed books are the much-preferred option. However, if you are studying at a distance, you are probably provided with ebooks and other digital documents. Other than buying the books yourself, the only option would be to print out elements of your required reading on your own printer as you won't have easy access to the university library.

> QUICK TIP: If English is not your first language, using ebooks will be easier than printed books as you will find it easier to get portions of the text translated online quickly.

However, some publishers will not let you print out portions of the books you are reading online. This is because they rightly think that if you want a printed book, you can pay them for it. Besides, have you seen the cost of printer ink? According to the UK Consumers' Association, *Which?*, printer ink is amongst the most expensive of all liquids, being more expensive than vintage champagne or designer brand perfumes (*Which? Press Office*, 2020). A typical university textbook would cost around £20 in ink and a further £10 in paper. But for the £30, all you end up with is a pile of printed paper, and it would be easy to get the pages out of order. If you really want a printed book, it is often cheaper to buy it than print it yourself. And I've not even calculated the cost of electricity used in printing the book or the wear and tear on the printer itself. It's a false economy to print out ebooks.

However, printing out portions of them is a good idea as it can help you get to grips with particular theories, for instance, or enable you to better understand complex passages. Some of the ebook suppliers do allow you to print out a few pages at a time. Or they allow you to save pages as a PDF file, and then you can print that. Others do not allow printing or creating PDFs, so it will depend upon the ebook supplier your university uses. If your ebook supplier has disabled the printing option, the best thing to do is contact your university librarian. The library will have a photocopying licence which allows them to copy selected pages of textbooks. If you are not on campus, many university libraries will copy the relevant pages and post them to your address. I know at my university the library will do this or post actual books to students. It is always worth checking with your university library about the facilities and options available to you, especially if you prefer to see some items in print and you cannot print them out yourself.

If none of this is possible because your university does not offer printing and you do not want a printer yourself, then consider getting a tablet device. Research from Germany has shown that when people read from devices like paper format, the outcomes are much the same as reading from print (Kretzschmar et al., 2013). Tablet devices that have a screen size of around ten inches and that can be held in portrait mode are a similar size and format to a typical book. That means it is easier for our brains to cope, compared with reading from a 27-inch computer screen, not held in our hands, for instance. If you are not able to print anything, a 10-inch tablet is a reasonable alternative.

▶ GETTING THE MOST FROM EBOOKS

Printing ebooks is just one issue facing students who read materials online. However, reading ebooks online poses some other issues for students. Quite apart from the health and well-being issues of reading a large amount of materials from a computer screen, there are practical issues involved in using ebooks. Often these relate to not understanding the software. Each ebook provider has a range of features enabling you to do some useful things within the textbook. However, in my discussions with students who use online ebook readers, I am surprised how many of them have not explored what the software can do. Instead, they just start reading what they need, scrolling through the pages. This can waste time and can also reduce the value the book provides. The most popular online academic ebook readers, such as Kortext, Perlego, and Vital Source, provide various features to enhance the ebooks they make available. Common to each of these services is the ability to highlight passages, add notes to specific items within the book, and bookmark specific pages to quickly return to them. In some ebook readers, you can also change the type size, the colour of the background, and the page's orientation so that you can have it presented in the best way for you to read. You will also find the ebook readers allow you to store references so that you can copy and paste relevant citations into your assignments. In addition, Kortext and Vital Source both include the option for the book to be read aloud to you. That way, it becomes an audiobook, providing you with some respite from having to sit at your screen and read.

QUICK TIP: *Get to know the hidden features of your ebook software, as there will be options available to help improve your online reading.*

▶ USE AUDIOBOOKS

Many popular books are available in audio format. However, few academic textbooks are made available this way. That's probably because they tend to be considerably longer than a typical paperback, so the production costs would make them expensive. If you have an ebook reader that includes "text to speech" facilities, then it may be worthwhile using that. There are also several similar standalone apps and online services that offer "read aloud" features. Much of this software is freely available, and you may find that such programs will improve your online learning. Some studies show that comprehension is increased in students who use audiobooks (Kartal and Simsek, 2017; Mohamed, 2018). Admittedly, these studies were only in students learning English as a foreign language, but it does indicate that audio can help increase understanding.

Furthermore, one study has shown that having audio available can increase the amount of leisure reading that university students undertake (Jansen, 2019). Raising the amount of reading you do is important. Many studies have shown a clear link between the time spent on reading books and students' writing ability. The more you read, the higher your marks. However, reading is time-consuming, and this is where audio versions or text-to-speech software can help. You can "read" using audio while doing something else, such as working out in the gym or taking the bus to the student union building.

For someone studying online, the use of audiobooks or text-to-speech software becomes more essential than for traditional students. In a real-world lecture theatre, lectures may supplement their teaching using handouts or copies of journal articles. Traditional students will get to see more printed items than those learning at a distance. When you are studying online, you don't get the chance to visit the library to check books, nor do you get those physical handouts provided to students in lecture theatres. For online students, everything is just a click away. That's nice and convenient. However, it also means you have considerably less printed material to read than traditional students. The rise in online reading materials means you can get more tired, and hence anything you can do to reduce the impact of online-only reading, the better it is for you and your well-being. That's why online students need to consider options such as text-to-speech as it will make studying online more manageable and more enjoyable. Even so, audiobooks are not replacements for textbooks. You can't make notes or highlight critical passages, for example. So, audiobooks and text-to-speech software should be seen as a way of enhancing your reading and not replacing it. For students with dyslexia or other difficulties such as any of the attention deficit disorders, reading online can be troublesome, and this is where audio versions can be of real help.

▶ CURATING YOUR READING

One of the problems with the amount of online reading you will do is remembering where it is all located. You will not want to add bookmarks to your web browser as it will become cluttered and unusable before long. You will need something to collect together all your reading materials. Otherwise, you will find it difficult when you need to revise or have to complete an assignment. With traditional studying, you would probably keep notes and printouts in a folder, perhaps with a different coloured folder for each subject you study. With online reading material, that is difficult. However, there are some ways in which you can achieve this. In the jargon of the online world, you need to "curate" your "content".

Various software programs can help you achieve this. Personally, I prefer a program called Evernote. All of the reading that I have completed in the research for this book, for example, is curated into a single "notebook" on Evernote called "Studying Online". I have tagged each of the items with relevant keywords and chapter numbers. That means I can find everything I need when I am writing specific elements of this book. You could save all the reading together for specific subjects and tag them for assignments, for example.

With Evernote, you can add PDFs, links to web pages, audio notes and handwritten items, and type your own material. You can find out more about notetaking with Evernote in Chapter 4. In terms of online reading, though, programs like Evernote allow you to organise all your reading materials in much the same way as you would do with paper documents within folders. Alternatives to Evernote include programs such as Microsoft OneNote and Notion. Both of these are popular with students. Indeed, Microsoft OneNote is included with the Microsoft 365 suite of office software which is given to many students. Plus, Microsoft OneNote includes a "Class Notebook" feature that allows lecturers to set up a series of notebooks to accompany lectures. As a result, you may find this embedded within many online study programs. However, all of these programs work in much the same way allowing you to collect your reading materials together.

Another way you might like to curate your reading materials is to use software that is focused upon the online reading you will do. There are various browser add-ons or extensions that can curate all the online reading into collections to save you from having to bookmark everything. Popular programs that can achieve this are Pocket and Flipboard, which can both help you store all the online reading materials you access in one place.

> **QUICK TIP: Choose software that will allow you to collect all your online reading materials into one place, such as "content curation" programs.**

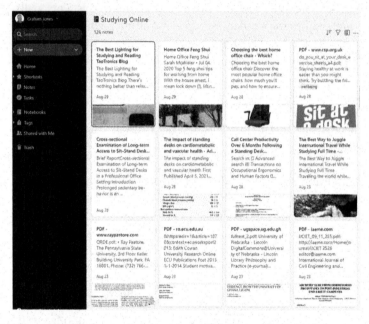

Figure 3.2 Reading material curated within Evernote

PRACTICAL TIPS

- **Take breaks.** Reading online is tiring. It's better to read in small sessions of around 15 minutes at a time. Take a rest for several minutes between each short reading session to help your eyes and improve concentration.
- **Use music.** Try listening to instrumental background music while reading. For many people, it can improve concentration and comprehension, especially if you use noise-cancelling head-phones.
- **Print important items.** Print out pages that are complex or which have fundamental theories you need to learn. If the ebook

doesn't let you print, ask the university library to provide you with photocopies from the printed version of the ebook.

- **Use text-to-speech software.** Get text-to-speech software to help reduce the vast volume of online reading you will need to complete. Such software can read aloud web pages and documents while you listen carefully and make notes.
- **File your reading.** Get content curation software so that you can file away and organise your online reading in much the same way as you would use folders to do that with printed documents.

▶ REFERENCES

Bernard, M., Liao, C.H. and Mills, M. (2001) 'MM: The Effects of Font Type and Size on the Legibility and Reading Time of Online Text by Older Adults', in *Vol. II Proceedings of ACM CHI 2001*. New York: ACM Press, pp. 175–176.

Buswell, G.T. (1947) 'The Subvocalization Factor in the Improvement of Reading', *The Elementary School Journal*, 48(4), pp. 190–196.

Clinton, V. (2019) 'Reading from Paper Compared to Screens: A Systematic Review and Meta-Analysis', *Journal of Research in Reading*, 42(2), pp. 288–325.

Crowder, R.G. and Wagner, R.K. (1992) *The Psychology of Reading*. New York: Oxford University Press.

Dewar, M., Alber, J., Butler, C., Cowan, N. and Della Sala, S. (2012) 'Brief Wakeful Resting Boosts New Memories over the Long Term', *Psychological Science*, 23(9) pp. 955–960.

Jansen, A. (2019) 'Increasing Leisure Reading among University Students Using e-Readers with Audio | Jansen | College & Research Libraries'. Available at: https://doi.org/10.5860/crl.80.3.356 (Accessed: 16 September 2021).

Kartal, G. and Simsek, H. (2017) 'The Effects of Audiobooks on EFL Students' Listening Comprehension', *The Reading Matrix: An International Online Journal*, 17(1), pp. 112–123.

Kretzschmar, F., Pleimling, D., Hosemann, J., Füssel, S., Bornkessel-Schlesewsky, I. and Schlesewsky, M. (2013) 'Subjective Impressions Do Not Mirror Online Reading Effort: Concurrent EEG-Eyetracking Evidence from the Reading of Books and Digital Media', *PLOS ONE*, 8(2), p. e56178.

Lehmann, J.A.M. and Seufert, T. (2017) 'The Influence of Background Music on Learning in the Light of Different Theoretical Perspectives and the Role of Working Memory Capacity', *Frontiers in Psychology*, 8, p. 1902.

Mohamed, M.M.K. (2018) 'Using Audiobooks for Developing Listening Comprehension among Saudi EFL Preparatory Year Students', *Journal of Language Teaching and Research*, 9(1), pp. 64–73.

Oliver, M.D., Levy, J.J. and Baldwin, D.R. (2021) 'Examining the Effects of Musical Type and Intensity in Performing the Flanker Task: A Test of Attentional Control Theory Applied to Non-Emotional Distractions', *Psychology of Music*, 49(4), pp. 1017–1026.

Pernice, K., Whitenton, K. and Nielsen, J. (2014) *How People Read on the Web: The Eyetracking Evidence*. Fremont, CA: Nielsen Norman Group.

Slowiaczek, M.L. and Clifton, C. (1980) 'Subvocalization and Reading for Meaning', *Journal of Verbal Learning and Verbal Behavior*, 19(5), pp. 573–582.

Which? Press Office (2020) 'Inkonceivably Expensive – Printer Ink Pricier than 32-Year-Old Scotch Whisky'. Available at: http://press. which.co.uk/whichpressreleases/inkonceivably-expensive-printer-ink-pricier-than-32-year-old-scotch-whisky (Accessed: 5 September 2021).

Yan, G., Meng, Z., Liu, N., He, L. and Paterson, K.B. (2018) 'Effects of Irrelevant Background Speech on Eye Movements during Reading', *Quarterly Journal of Experimental Psychology*, 71(6), pp. 1270–1275.

4

Online notetaking

Taking good notes is a fundamental part of studying. Whether you are in a lecture, reading a textbook, or researching online, you will be taking notes. Indeed, in an article about notetaking in *The Guardian* newspaper, the writer Harry Slater said that "university is 95% notetaking". He added, "If you can take good notes, you're on track to make the academic side of things much easier for yourself.[1]" During your time at university, you will make lots of notes, and I mean lots ...! In a typical module, you will take notes for around 40 hours of lectures, 12 chapters of textbooks, and a host of other literature and websites. Over the course of your degree, you will cover about 18 different modules. That's a great deal of material on which you will take notes. When you leave university, you will be able to wallpaper several rooms with all the notes you took.

One of the problems for university students is that they have rarely been taught how to take notes. A study on notetaking in New Zealand found that most students learn notetaking through "trial and error" (van der Meer, 2012). Indeed, in my discussions with students, I often find that it is just as students are about to leave university that they have discovered the best way of taking

DOI: 10.4324/9781003259695-6

notes that works for them. "If only I knew this when I started" is a common feeling amongst many university students. Of course, universities do provide study skills advice. Their websites are full of information on all kinds of topics to help students with their studies, including notetaking. However, students are frequently left to find this out for themselves while the academics get on with teaching the actual subjects.

Meanwhile, students become confused as to the best way to take notes. They will ask one lecturer who will talk about the "best notetaking system" while another lecturer will dismiss that idea and say that an alternative is "clearly the ultimate method". You can also find several discussions on student forums, such as "The Student Room", which had over 1,300 posts discussing notetaking when I wrote this chapter. It is clearly a popular topic, but the advice and suggestions on those forums is also just as varied as the information you get from lecturers. One of the reasons why students only find the best notetaking system after trial and error is that it is a personal thing. What works for one person does not suit another. My method of taking notes is not likely to suit you unless you think the same way as me. All we really know is that students who take plenty of well-structured notes are the ones who do best. So, it is a good idea to get all the trial and error over and done with as quickly as possible so that the bulk of your studies will have excellent notes.

> QUICK TIP: Experiment with various notetaking methods at the outset of your studies to find one that works best for you.

▶ NOTETAKING METHODS AND SYSTEMS

Most people who make notes simply start writing things down on paper, scribbling reminders of what was said in a lecture, or summarising the material they have been reading. It is the most popular method of taking notes, but also the least efficient. It is difficult to find things in an endless stream of scribbles. Often, you can find it hard to read what you have written. Plus, the lack of structure means it is hard to extract meaning from your notes. The only real benefit of writing random notes appears to be that it helps your memory and subsequent recall. The act of writing things down provides the brain with additional processing for a particular item. This helps you form memories. So, random note-taking does have value. However, compared with more structured notetaking, that single value is relatively small.

Cornell Notes

The Cornell Method of taking notes was developed in the 1950s by Professor Walter Pauk, who worked at Cornell University, New

Figure 4.1 The basic layout for Cornell Notes

York. He later popularised the method in his book *How to Study in College*, which was first published in 1962 and continued through 11 editions until his death in 2019 (Pauk and Owens, 2014). The Cornell Method divides a sheet of paper into three distinct areas: the cue column, the main notetaking column, and the summary box (see Figure 4.1).

The system requires you to make brief notes of the lecture or reading material in the main column for the notes. Then, once you have finished taking notes, you enter some "cues" in the first column. These are questions that help establish connections or jog your memory. After you have written these cues, you should then summarise the entire page of notes in a couple of sentences in the summary box. You can download a Cornell Notes template from the website I have created to accompany this book, https://study ingonline.tips. Because Cornell Notetaking is structured, it means that it is easy for online students to use. You can use templates within Microsoft Word or Google Docs, for example, to produce your notes. You could even create a template for filing systems such as Evernote®, Microsoft OneNote, Nimbus Note, or Notion.

This method of notetaking has been studied many times and has been shown to be of help to a wide range of students. In 2008, a study was announced at an educational conference that showed the Cornell Method was mainly of use where knowledge had to be synthesised or where evaluation was necessary (Jacobs, 2008). The researchers found that when acquiring knowledge was required, an alternative method of taking notes was better. This method is known as "guided notetaking".

Guided notetaking

Guided notetaking is where you add to existing notes, usually provided by your lecturer. These notes outline a lecture or summarise an area of research or some reading material. You can read those notes to accompany the lecture or textbook and then annotate them with additional information that will help you understand the essentials. For my students, I provide them with some notes on Microsoft OneNote. They can add to these with highlights, comments, underlines, and so on. See Figures 4.2 and 4.3.

Figure 4.2 A set of notes for students to annotate

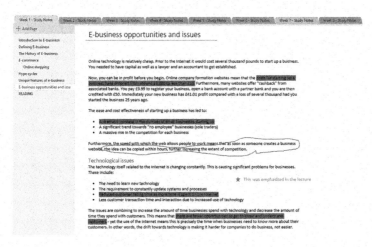

Figure 4.3 An annotated set of notes

For people studying online, guided notetaking is particularly help-ful. Lecturers provide summary notes in electronic form, and stu-dents can then add to those notes with annotations and additional notes of their own. However, one of the problems with guided notes is that you are dependent upon lecturers creating the notes in the first place. Furthermore, if the lecturer's notes don't click with you because they write notes in a different way to you, then you will find it harder to use them.

Mind maps

Another prevalent method of notetaking for students is mind mapping. This is a highly visual method of making notes. You can see an example of a simple mind map in Figure 4.4 which is the summary mind map of this chapter.

Traditionally, you start your mind map with a central idea in the middle and then start drawing lines for each idea with a few words to remind you of the information. The lines start at the one o'clock position and then go clockwise around the central concept. They have very few words on them, as the mind map is meant to be a trigger to remind you of stored memories. However, people do

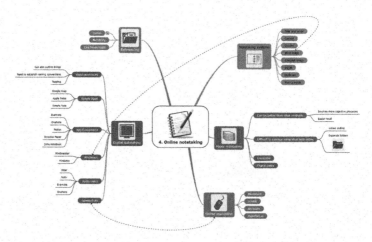

Figure 4.4 A sample mind map

add detail to their mind maps when they use online mind mapping software. This detail can be hidden by the software so that you merely see the overall visual effect, only being able to view the details when you click on the appropriate button. When drawing mind maps, you are encouraged to use pictures and different colours as well as symbols and emojis as these help recall. Many studies have been conducted showing the benefits of mind maps. However, not everyone likes them, especially students who think sequentially rather than visually. Even so, research has shown that mind maps increase the motivation to learn (Aleksić et al., 2011). Hence they are worth considering, even if your main notes are constructed separately. The use of mind maps can help you consolidate information and make the subject appear "whole" as the map summarises an entire topic.

> QUICK TIP: Even if you think you won't like mind maps, give them a trial. Once people have used mind maps for even a short while, they often see value in them.

Concept maps

A concept map is similar to a mind map. Indeed, most of the mind mapping software programs can also create concept maps. The critical difference, though, is that a concept map is hierarchical. In addition, concept maps are text-only with no imagery. As a result, a concept map is helpful to see the relationships between items and topics. You can see a concept map in Figure 4.5. For online learning, you may find that a concept map is best used as a revision aid rather than a notetaking method for learning new material. It is the kind of diagram that you can produce once you understand a topic.

SQ3R notes

Another form of notetaking that is popular with university students is known as "SQ3R". This stands for Survey, Question, Read,

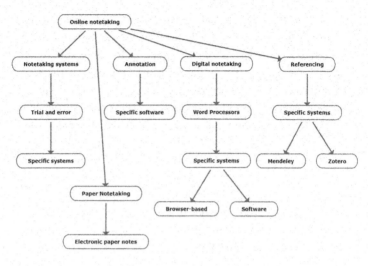

Figure 4.5 A concept map

Recite, Review. You can download an SQ3R notes template from the website I have created to accompany this book, https://study ingonline.tips. This form of notetaking is best reserved for making notes from written material rather than lectures. However, you could use the technique if your lectures are recorded and you are watching videos. The first step is to conduct a "survey" in which you skim through the material to identify the structure and important elements, such as figures and tables. Then you write down some questions about the material based on the headings and subheadings. After that, you read the material, all the while looking for answers to your questions. When you get an answer, you "recite" it by writing that down. After that, you write a summary of the information you have gained in the review section of your notes. This method of notetaking has been shown to help students gain higher marks in exams (Carlston, 2011). So it is worthwhile considering.

Outlining

This is probably the most common form of taking notes. You write a heading for the section of the lecture or the textbook, then you write a number of bullet points under that main item. You repeat this for each of the topics covered in the lecture. If you were to look at a fellow student's notebook, this is the most likely form of notes you would see. For students studying online, word processors, such as Microsoft Word, have outlining features built-in. So it is easy to create digital outlines of lectures and textbook chapters. However, there is an issue with outline notes or linear notes as they are sometimes called. It is challenging to find material in them. If you need to locate something specific within your notes, a stream of bullet points makes it more cumbersome to see what you want. As a result, when revising for exams or finding information for assignments, going back over outline notes can take additional time.

Matrix notes

Matrix notetaking is where you divide a topic into sections, and each one of those has a box on a page. This is particularly useful

Notetaking systems	Paper notetaking	Digital notetaking
Trial and error	Better than digital	Word processors
Cornell	More cognitive	Notetaking apps
Guided	processes	Note ecosystems
Mind maps	Difficult to integrate	Mind maps
Concept maps	online	Audio notes
SQ3R	Digital paper	Screenshots
Outlines	Livescribe™	
Matrix notes		
Annotations	Referencing	
Annotated	Zotero	
screenshots	Mendeley	
Mindstone	Cite them right	
Scrible		
Annotate		
Hypothesis		

Figure 4.6 A matrix note

for book chapters, for example. You can divide the chapter into themes or concepts and then make notes in each of the matrix sections. In the example in Figure 4.6, you will see this chapter summarised in matrix note format. You should be able to see that the entire chapter is concisely noted in such a way that you can easily pinpoint specific items.

Rather like concept maps, matrix notes tend to work best when you have studied a topic, and you want to revise it. They are also very useful in drawing together ideas for an assignment. You can easily produce matrix notes in a word processor. Figure 4.6 was created in Microsoft Word using the "Insert table" feature.

▶ PAPER NOTETAKING FOR ONLINE STUDYING

Whatever form of notes you want to keep, it might seem odd that I would suggest that you should make your notes on paper when you are studying online. However, that is precisely what I am going to suggest. There is a place for digital notetaking, as you will discover later in this chapter. However, just because you are studying online does not mean you should give up pen and paper.

In his review of the literature on notetaking, the American psychologist Michael Friedman says that when people type notes, they tend to focus their efforts on the production of the notes rather than thinking about the information (Friedman, 2014). Indeed, research does suggest that when students sit typing as they watch lectures or read materials online, they tend to just type what they hear or what they are reading. There is little thinking going on because all the mental effort is spent on typing as much as possible. I remember giving a lecture in the Vinson Auditorium at the University of Buckingham when a student asked me to stop and repeat what I had just said. I asked, "Sorry, didn't I make it clear?" The student responded, "It's not about you being clear, you were just speaking quickly, and I couldn't type everything you said". Rather than listening to establish understanding, the student was listening to merely type what I was saying. When students were moved to online-only lectures due to the Covid-19 pandemic, I recall one of them saying how grateful they were that the lectures were now all on video. "Why is that?", I asked. "It's because it means I can stop and start the recording so that I can type everything you say. I couldn't have done that in a live lecture, so the recordings are great". When studying using a computer, it is too easy to think that notetaking is just typing up what you have been listening to or reading. The problem, though, is that your mind focuses on the creation of the notes. When you take notes on paper, there is a greater tendency to listen, think, interpret, and then make the notes. When people are making notes on paper, they tend not to write things down verbatim. This gives them the mental opportunity to process the information rather than just record it.

Researchers at Washington University in St Louis, USA, carried out a set of experiments investigating digital notetaking (Bui, My-erson, and Hale 2013). This series of experiments showed that when students just took down everything that was said in a lecture, their ability to recall information dropped off after 24 hours. The students who had been asked to type up structure notes, though, had a more long-lasting recollection of the lecture content. This suggests that it is not necessarily the use of a computer to make notes that is the potential problem. Rather, it is the kind of notes that you take on a computer. If all you do is type up what you hear in a lecture or read in a book, your short-term memory is excellent for the material you have studied. However, that memory effect reduces over time. Hence, if you really do want to use your laptop to type up lecture notes, then you will gain a better understanding of the subject if you use one of the structured notetaking methods rather than just typing what you hear.

QUICK TIP: *If you would rather type up notes instead of hand-writing them, then use structured notes rather than linear notes as you will gain more from the structure.*

It is worth noting that other studies have found different findings regarding digital notetaking. For example, a study conducted at Princeton University, USA, showed that when students typed notes, they had lower comprehension than students who used handwritten notes (Mueller and Oppenheimer, 2014). Taken together with the studies about recall from notes, studies suggest that you can remember more when you type up structured notes, but your understanding of that material is less than when you handwrite them. When you take notes on your computer, you can remember more but have less understanding of a topic than if you had handwritten them. Given that a degree is about understanding, rather than remembering, it suggests you should not give up on handwritten notes just yet.

▶ INTEGRATING PAPER NOTES

If you do take notes on paper, there is an added problem when studying online. Much of what you study will be in digital format. If you have notes on paper, it becomes more challenging to integrate your notes with your online study resources. In the days when all studying was face to face, and there were no digital materials, it was easy to integrate your notes. For example, you could photocopy relevant textbook pages and put them in a folder together with your handwritten lecture notes. That's not easy these days if your textbook is an ebook and you have taken handwritten notes of a lecture that is connected with the topic of one of the book's chapters. This is why so many students prefer to take notes on their laptops. It means they can integrate their lecture notes with the other digital materials more efficiently. However, as you have seen already, there are problems with typed notes. They help you remember, but they can sometimes hamper understanding. Handwritten notes appear to be superior for developing understanding.

A degree is about demonstrating your level of critical thinking. All university degrees are graded, showing the level of critical thinking that you have demonstrated. The higher the classification of your degree, the greater your level of critical thinking. To think critically, though, you need to understand the topic and be able to think about it. Getting a degree is not a memory test. Instead, it is a test of understanding. Hence, typed notes may hamper your chances of getting the best degree you can achieve as they tend to help memory more than they help thinking. But you can't achieve high levels of critical thinking if your handwritten notes are separated from your other learning materials. They need to be integrated. Otherwise, you will waste time going between digital and handwritten items. Also, you will not be able to spot the connections between materials as easily.

Colour coding handwritten notes

One way you can integrate handwritten notes with your digital materials is to use colour coding. You could choose specific colours for each topic or theme and then store your handwritten notes in a folder of the same colour. You could then colour-code your digital folders and documents to match. On an Apple Mac, you can do this easily as it is built into the operating system. It is a little cumbersome, but plenty of instruction videos on YouTube demonstrate how to do this. Alternatively, you will find instructions on how to change folder colours on a Mac on the website I have created to accompany this book, https://study ingonline.tips. If you have a Windows computer, colour-coding folders are not built into the system, so you will need to download software to allow you to do this. You will find a list of programs at https://studyingonline.tips.

Once you have set up colour-coded folders on your computer and have matching physical folders for your handwritten notes and other printed materials, it will be easier to find relevant information. For instance, you may be checking something in a green folder on the PC, so all you need to do is open the matching physical folder to find relevant notes.

Use digital paper for notes

One way you can integrate your handwritten notes with your digital files is to create handwritten notes using digital paper. There are various ways in which you can do this, but it means that you can write on paper, and your notes are then converted into digital files, which you can then attach to the information you have stored on your computer.

One of the most popular methods of digital notetaking is a system called Livescribe™. This is a special pen that uses specific paper in notepads or notebooks. The pen and the paper work together so that the system records precisely where on the page a particular note was made. It can also record the audio of a lecture and connect a specific note at a particular point with the relevant time in the sound file. As a result, you can press on the page and listen to what was being said at the precise time you made that note. The handwritten notes are also converted by software to appear on your computer or mobile device app. Several studies of the use of Livescribe™ have shown it to be of benefit to students. For example, research at Southern Connecticut State University found that students who used Livescribe™ for notetaking had improved focus and higher performance (Tucker and Zamfir, 2021). Studies have also shown that for students with dyslexia and other learning difficulties, digital notetaking systems like Livescribe™ can be of significant help (Belson, Hartmann, and Sherman, 2013).

However, other digital notetaking systems do not require special paper. These allow you to use any notepad or notebook. When writing your notes, you attach a small camera-based device to the top of the page. You then write your notes with the special pen, and the system can track what you are writing. Like Livescribe™, these systems convert your notes to digital form, allowing you to store your handwritten notes together with all your other computer-based notes and resources.

An alternative is to buy a special notepad that has special marks on it to allow you to store your notes digitally when you snap a picture of each page. Both Moleskine® and Oxford have notebooks in their range which allow you to store handwritten notes digitally. Oxford comes with its own app called Scribzee®. However, these are not automatic systems – you have to remember to take a picture of each page of notes. Even so, they are a cost-effective way of storing handwritten notes in digital form. If you use Microsoft Office, an even cheaper way is to use the Lens app. This allows you to snap pictures of your handwritten notes and store them in a relevant folder in your OneDrive system or within a OneNote document. This allows you to integrate handwritten notes with your online information easily. However, you have to remember to take pictures of all your notes, and if you have several pages, it can take extra time that you can avoid if you have a fully digital system such as a digital pen.

> **QUICK TIP:** *You can integrate handwritten notes with digital ones relatively easily, but you have to think about how you will do this and have a plan.*

Handwrite notes on a digital device

There are now several digital devices that offer you a paper-like feel when writing. These look like tablet devices, but they are dedicated to notetaking. They do not offer the other features of Android™ tablets or the iPad®. However, if you want to handwrite notes and ensure they are available digitally without having to remember to take a picture, these devices can be beneficial. Two well-known brands are Remarkable and Supernote. They are designed to feel like paper when you write on them, allowing you to get handwritten notes on a digital device.

You can also handwrite on a standard tablet device. However, it can feel as though you are writing on glass or a shiny surface and getting the same degree of control over your handwriting is not easy. However, there are several manufacturers of screen protectors which claim to provide the surface of your tablet with a paper-like feel so that you can write by hand. If you already have a tablet device, you may wish to buy one of these screen protectors to test out handwriting. They are relatively expensive and can cost as much as five times the amount of a regular screen protector. Even so, that is still going to be cheaper than buying a dedicated device and they are cheap enough for you to test out handwriting on your tablet.

Whether you use your own tablet, get a digital handwriting pad, use a digital notepad and pen, or just take pictures of your handwritten notes, several options are available to you. Ultimately, there are options available to you so that you can integrate your handwritten notes with your digital files. You ought to consider what will work best for you and the way you work taking into account your budget. If you integrate your handwritten notes with your digital files from the outset of studying online, you will find it much easier to get on with your studies. Just imagine when it comes to exam time, and you have to work your way through your online files and your handwritten notes and try to work out how they are all connected. That problem can be avoided if you set up an integrated system for handwritten and digital materials from the outset.

▶ DIGITAL ANNOTATION

Whenever I walk into a lecture theatre, I can see the students who have been working hard on their studies. They have their textbooks in front of them, and I can see sticky note bookmarks sticking out. If they have the book open, I will see various passages highlighted as well as some scribbled notes in the margins. If I have provided lecture notes in advance, I will see the same. Students who have read the notes in advance will have annotated what I had written and highlighted some particular points. Just looking around the lecture theatre and seeing who has annotated their textbooks and notes gives me a clue as to who will do well with the assessments ...!

Writing notes in the margins, highlighting key points, and underlining relevant passages is an integral part of studying. Students have been doing it for years. However, doing that when materials are online is complex or cumbersome. The ebook suppliers do allow you to make notes and highlight passages, as explained in Chapter 3. You will, however, be encountering a great deal of material that is not in an ebook system. There will be web pages, documents that you download, PDFs that you view online, and so on.

Annotating PDFs

If you wish to annotate PDFs, the software that comes with your computer may not be able to do this. This was mentioned in a set of interviews with students by the software company Wondershare, the manufacturers of PDFelement. A San Francisco student said, "I need to annotate the text clearly and concisely, but the default PDF editor on my laptop was not capable of annotation, reading scanned texts and other functions. It made completing work for my courses difficult" (Wondershare, 2021). This is a common finding. Students want to annotate the PDFs they have to read but cannot do so unless they purchase additional software. You will find a list of suitable PDF programs at the website I have created to accompany this book, https://studyingonline.tips.

Annotating web pages

Much of what you read online will be in the form of web pages. Annotating these can be difficult. For instance, you may need to save the web page, convert it to PDF, and then annotate it. That takes time. There are two main ways you can annotate and add notes to web pages:

1. Take a screenshot and annotate it
2. Get specialist browser extensions that allow you to save annotated pages.

Computers come with screenshot software; however, their features are limited. Often, they cannot capture a scrolling web page, nor can they add text or highlights to the page. If you wish to use screenshots to capture what you are reading online, you will need additional software beyond what is provided on the computer itself. As a lecturer, I need to store many screenshots and annotate them to share with students. I use a program called Snagit by the company Techsmith. This has extensive features for annotating and highlighting, and the company has specialised in the education sector with its software. Hence, for students, this program could be appealing, especially as the program is offered at a discount for people who have an email address from an educational establishment. Other programs are listed at the website I have created to accompany this book, https://studyingonline.tips.

If you would prefer to work directly in your web browser and not have to swap to a screenshot program, then you can consider browser plugins that allow for annotation. Many of these are available; however, there are three worthy of particular consideration as they allow you to annotate PDFs in addition to web pages. These services are called Mindstone, Scrible, and Hypothes.is. These allow you to annotate and add notes to web pages and upload PDFs or view a PDF in a web browser tab and annotate that as well. All of the annotations and PDFs are stored in your account with these services. Some elements are free, but if you wish to take advantage of the full range of options, you will need to pay for the premium versions of the programs.

> **QUICK TIP:** Annotating web pages, PDFs, and other documents will enhance your learning and help your memory and understanding.

▶ MAKING NOTES DIGITALLY

Even though you may well handwrite some notes, it is inevitable with online studying that you will also make notes digitally in addition to annotating what you read on the web. Many students that I teach use word processors to write their notes up.

However, this can be rather cumbersome, and unless you have a truly remarkable memory, it can be challenging to find information amongst an extensive list of documents.

Making notes with word processors

Word processors have a range of features that allow you to use them more effectively for notetaking. One way is to switch to "Outline" mode, rather than the typical "Typewriter" mode, or "Print Layout". In Microsoft Word, click on the "View" menu option and then on "Outline". Alternatively, type Ctrl + Alt + O, and you will switch to the Outline view. For Google Docs, you will find the outlining option also in the View menu. A word processor outline allows you to write bullet point style notes, but move them around easily and add text annotations and highlighting.

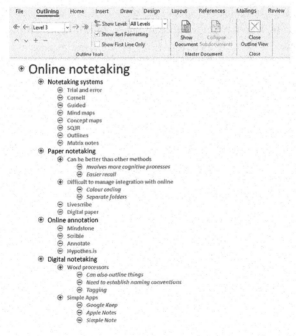

Figure 4.7 A word processor outline in Microsoft Word

Another feature of Microsoft Word that is useful for notetaking is the tagging feature. When you save the file, there is the option to add a "tag". You can provide a tag that allows you to find notes easily by searching for tags.

However, there is little to recommend a word processor as a notetaking system. The fact that Microsoft has produced a program called Microsoft OneNote, which is explicitly designed to take notes, should be a clear indication that a word processor alone is not a proper notetaking system.

> QUICK TIP: If you have Microsoft 365, use OneNote for digital notetaking rather than Microsoft Word.

Using note ecosystems for digital notetaking

Microsoft OneNote is an "ecosystem", allowing you to collate all of your notes together in one place. In addition, you can use Microsoft OneNote as a note filing system, making it easy to co-ordinate and integrate all of your work and resources. The main competitor to Microsoft OneNote is a program called Evernote®. Students also like Notion or another notetaking system called Nimbus Note or Zoho Notebook. These are complete systems with a wide range of features. You can use them as a simple note-book, typing up your notes on your lectures and what you have been reading. However, there is much more to these ecosystems than a straightforward notebook. You can add pictures, videos, and audio files. You can insert other documents such as word processor files or PDFs. You can then annotate what you have imported into the notebooks. You can also import handwritten notes, either as images captured via your phone or by import-ing files from your digital pen application, for example. Moles-kine® also produces a notebook that is integrated with Evernote®, providing a more direct way of inserting handwritten notes into your digital notebooks.

> **QUICK TIP:** *Sign up for trials of each of these notetaking ecosystems. That way, you can experiment and compare the features to determine which one works best for you.*

It is worthwhile trying out each of these notetaking ecosystems so that you can compare them and discover the variety of features on offer. One thing that will quickly become apparent is that you can use these systems to store everything associated with your studies. You can download lecture notes, insert lecturer video files, add your own notes, and also record online live lectures and include the audio file. You will be given access to a wide range of study resources, and these ecosystems can collate them together and allow you to add your own notes as well. Furthermore, these systems all come with "web capture" extensions for web browsers. That means you can take screenshots of entire web pages (even the ones that scroll) and annotate them. As if this were not enough to impress you, the manufacturers of these systems also have apps for mobile devices. As a result, you can access your notes and all of the associated files anywhere. You do not have to be at your computer. In addition, whether you are using these systems on your main computer or on a mobile device, you can search for any word, and it will be found both within your own notes and in the documents that you have added. For online students, this is a significant advantage as it enables you to find everything associated with a particular idea. Using one of these ecosystems will save you a considerable amount of time when you need to locate information to help with an assignment, for example. As an aside, all of the notes for this book were compiled in an Evernote® notebook, together with all of the research references, PDFs, and web pages that I used. Everything associated with this book is available for me to search in one place, together will all my annotations and notes. I could have done the same thing in any of the other notetaking ecosystems. Ultimately, which one you select is down to personal choice.

Simple notetaking apps

There are dozens of notetaking apps available, either for mobile devices or as software for computers. Popular ones include Apple Notes, Google Keep, and Simplenote. These are great for making very quick notes, such as reminders or lists. You could use one of these apps to jot down ideas, for example, or to list recommended reading. They do not have the functionality of an ecosystem like Microsoft OneNote or Evernote. However, they do have value. For example, you may be working on an assignment in a group, and you need to jot down some quick reminders of your tasks. Or you could be chatting to friends on a video call, and someone recommends a good book to read. You could quickly make a note in one of these apps rather than loading up an ecosystem just to jot down a few words.

> QUICK TIP: *Have a notetaking app on your mobile phone so that you can jot down ideas and reminders.*

▶ USING AUDIO NOTES

Even though you may be studying alone, at a distance to the university, there will be a reasonable amount of audio to which you will need to listen. Some lectures, for example, will be in audio only, rather like a podcast. Indeed, some lecturers – including me – have a podcast that is recommended listening for students. You can import such audio files and links to recordings into your notetaking system. However, you can also make audio notes yourself. Sometimes this is easier for students when they are listening to audio as their mind is in "audio mode". For instance, while listening to a podcast, you can record a quick audio note on your mobile phone voice recording app. Some students that I teach also prefer to record audio notes, summarising what they are reading in a textbook, for example.

Audio notes can be handy for revision when it comes to exam time. You can playback your audio summary of a textbook chapter to help you remember what you read. Indeed, if you have audio notes like this, you can revise while you are in the gym or walking down the road to the pub ...! However, there is a problem with audio notes. Finding what you want within them can be time-consuming. This is where transcription software can come in useful. Services such as Otter.ai and Notiv can take your audio file and turn it into text. They can also monitor online video calls, for example, and transcribe them. This means that you will have a text-based version of the audio files you have recorded. These text files can be more easily searched than an audio file. You can add the audio and the transcription to your notetaking system, and there you will be able to search for specific elements you might need. Both Otter.ai and Notiv have free options for students.

▶ KEEPING NOTE OF REFERENCES

All academic work requires references. They show where you obtained the information and allow your readers to check the integrity of what you are saying. Your essays, reports, and other assignments will all need referencing. Whenever I talk with students about referencing, I realise that they waste a great deal of time on it. That's because they don't store or note down references accurately in the first place. When it comes to writing their assignment, they often have to look up their sources again to write their list of references. Or they find that they haven't kept a note of their source, and they need to do the research all over again. The answer to this is to make a note of your references every time you access a source.

Some students jot down their references in a separate word processor document as they work on each assignment. The problem with this is that the document only applies to one assignment, and so if a source is used in more than one piece of work, the student has to recreate the reference all over again. Plus, searching for a reference across multiple word processor documents is time-consuming and not fun ...!

A better way of assembling references is to use reference software. There are two very popular methods of storing all your references. One is called Mendeley, and the other is Zotero. They both work in similar ways, so it is a subjective decision as to which one you prefer. Personally, I like Zotero, and all of the references for this book were compiled in it. However, I have lecturer colleagues at university who prefer Mendeley and can't get to grips with Zotero. It doesn't matter; choose one and use it.

The programs have web browser extensions so that when you are reading a source online, you can click on the button and add the source to your list, filing it appropriately according to the work you are doing. These extensions store all the relevant details, such as year of publication, author's name, the title of the paper, the name of the journal, and so on. When you need to produce your list of references at the end of your assignment, all you then do is press the appropriate menu option in Zotero or Mendeley, and your fully formatted reference list is created. You only need to tell it which referencing format you are using, and the program does all the hard work, saving you a great deal of time. For the reference list at the end of this chapter, all I had to do in Zotero was press the "Create Bibliography" option, confirm that I wanted to use the "Harvard" style of referencing and then click the OK button. I didn't have to concern myself as to which items were in italics, where the brackets went, or the order of each of the items. Zotero did all the work for me, saving me time and ensuring the formatting was correct. Students can lose marks if their referencing is incorrect, so a program like Zotero or Mendeley can ensure you get higher scores.

Some universities use a different system called Cite Them Right. This is a website that accompanies a book of the same name (Pears and Shields, 2019). Universities can subscribe to the system, and you would access this through your VLE. The system does not store references for you, though. It merely allows you to check that you have created the references correctly according to the format required by your discipline and faculty. Even if your university does subscribe to this, I would still recommend getting something like Zotero or Mendeley as you will be able to store and organise your references, something you cannot do at Cite Them Right.

QUICK TIP: *Try out Mendeley and Zotero and choose the one you like best. Then use it to store references for everything you read.*

One final point about keeping notes of your references and that is to avoid many of the websites that suggest they can help you create references. Some of these are inaccurate. Others are just crammed with advertising. And some I have seen appear rather flimsy, to say the least. Some are good and helpful for referencing in a hurry or when you do not have access to Zotero or Mendeley. However, if you want control over your references (and why wouldn't you), then choose one of those two programs.

PRACTICAL TIPS

- **Experiment with notetaking systems.** There is a variety of systems available for taking notes. Try as many as you can to find out which one works best for you. You might find that different systems are more suited to particular situations. You might like guided notes for lectures and mind maps or SQ3R for textbooks, for example.
- **Integrate handwritten notes.** Handwritten notes will help you learn more and understand things better. However, you need to integrate them with your digital materials to gain the most benefit. To do this, you can use your own system, perhaps based on colour coding. Or you can invest in additional technology such as a digital pen and paper system.
- **Select an annotation system.** You will need to annotate what you read online and make notes. With printed materials, this was easy. Online it can be cumbersome. You have various options for annotating things like PDFs and web pages. Choose the one that works best for you and the way you study.
- **Consider how you will store and organise digital notes.** Will you create your own system of folders and upload materials yourself? Or will you use a digital notetaking ecosystem? It doesn't matter much what you choose to do, but you need to choose something. Otherwise, your digital notes will be in a mess and finding things will be time-consuming and stressful.

▶ NOTE

1 Courtesy of Guardian News & Media Ltd.

▶ REFERENCES

Aleksić, V., Stanković, N., Papic, M. and Besic, C. (2011) 'The Evaluation of Using Mind Maps in Teaching', *Technics Technologies Education Management*, 6, pp. 337–343.

Belson, S.I., Hartmann, D. and Sherman, J. (2013) 'Digital Note Taking: The Use of Electronic Pens with Students with Specific Learning Disabilities', *Journal of Special Education Technology*, 28(2), pp. 13–24.

Bui, D.C., Myerson, J. and Hale, S. (2013) 'Note-Taking with Computers: Exploring Alternative Strategies for Improved Recall', *Journal of Educational Psychology*, 105(2), pp. 299–309.

Carlston, D.L. (2011) 'Benefits of Student-Generated Note Packets: A Preliminary Investigation of SQ3R Implementation', *Teaching of Psychology*, 38(3), pp. 142–146.

Friedman, M.C. (2014) *Notes on Note-Taking: Review of Research and Insights for Students and Instructors*. Harvard Initiative for Learning and Teaching. Cambridge, MA: Harvard University. Available at: https://hwpi.harvard.edu/files/hilt/files/notetaking_0.pdf (Accessed: 18 September 2021).

Jacobs, K. (2008) 'A Comparison of Two Note Taking Methods in a Secondary English Classroom'. In *Proceedings of the 4th Annual GRASP Symposium*, pp. 119–120. Wichita, KS: Wichita State University.

Mueller, P.A. and Oppenheimer, D.M. (2014) 'The Pen is Mightier than the Keyboard: Advantages of Longhand over Laptop Note Taking', *Psychological Science*, 25(6), pp. 1159–1168.

Pauk, W. and Owens, R. J. Q. (2014) *How to Study in College*, 11th edn. Boston, MA: Wadsworth Cengage Learning.

Pears, R. and Shields, G. (2019) *Cite Them Right*, 11th edn. London: Red Globe Press.

Slater, H. (2013) 'Students: How to Take Notes in Lectures', *The Guardian*, 29 April. Available at: www.theguardian.com/education/2013/apr/29/how-to-take-notes (Accessed: 17 September 2021).

Tucker, L. and Zamfir, B. (2021) 'Student Perception on the Impact of the Livescribe Smartpen as an Accommodation', Universal Access in the Information Society. DOI: 10.1007/s10209-021-00806-2 (Accessed: 19 September 2021).

van der Meer, J. (2012) 'Students' Notetaking Challenges in the Twenty-First Century: Considerations for Teachers and Academic Staff Developers', *Teaching in Higher Education*, 17(1), pp. 13–23.

Wondershare (2021) 'How Does an Online Course Student Make His Study Efficient?' Available at: https://pdf.wondershare.com/user-story/education-industry.html (Accessed: 19 September 2021).

5 Using study forums

I challenge you to visit any university campus, anywhere in the world and not be able to find groups of students huddled together chatting about their work. Whether they are in the coffee shop, in the library, or even in the student union bar, you are bound to find small groups of students discussing something about their studies. It's a natural occurrence. Students go to lectures and seminars, they read part of a textbook, and then they talk to each other. They might ask questions for clarification if they didn't quite understand something. They may well be sympathising with one another for finding the textbook hard going. Or they could be talking to each other about the forthcoming assignment, looking for ideas and tips to help them with their own work. Students inevitably chat with each other about their studies. In fact, you will find in most universities there are several places explicitly designed for the purpose. In the entrance to the Business School building where I work, there is a small area with comfy chairs and low coffee tables. The only function of this space is to allow students to sit and chat with one another. Across campus, in one of the lecture room buildings, there is a central space with sofas. Before and after lectures, I find students sitting there chatting, even though they are

DOI: 10.4324/9781003259695-7

only a short walk from their accommodation and could go home. Instead, they like to sit and chat.

Students who study at a distance do not have the opportunity to wander around campus and chat with other students. I have been an associate lecturer at the Open University in the UK since 1999. In the past, when I got a new group of students at the start of the academic year, one of my important tasks was to help with the formation of "study buddy groups". Open University students study at home, alone. They used to have lectures sent to them on video and on audiotapes. They were sent a series of textbooks in the post as well as several other documents. They had plenty to read, watch, and listen to. But they had no other students to talk with. Hence, my task was to help students find others who were doing the same course and who lived relatively local to them. Then I encouraged them to get together every week or two, suggesting they could meet over coffee or an evening drink. It was the Open University's way of helping distance learning students get a similar experience to campus-based students. Even though the Open University students could not informally bump into each other on campus, they could at least meet up and chat about their studies. Indeed, when I ran face-to-face tutorials with Open University students, I encouraged them to meet up after the lecture, perhaps going to a nearby pub. Or I said it might be an idea to arrive an hour before the timetabled time and grab a coffee together. It was my way of helping Open University students get as much interaction with other students as possible.

On campus, that interaction is always present. It helps students with their studies. Often it helps them confirm they understand the materials they are studying. Or it helps them clarify their thinking. Discussing your studies with other students can be a critical component of getting a degree. Indeed, research from the University of Natal in South Africa showed that informal groups of students discussing their studies can have positive impacts (Bertram, 2004). The research found that discussing studies with other students provided moral support as well as academic assistance. The study also showed that chatting with other students can be motivating.

Students often do not realise how much they learn from each other. Academics call it "peer learning", where you can learn new ideas and gain greater understanding from other students, rather than a lecturer. I am a psychologist, and this is no surprise to me. In the area of child development, the notion of learning from people around you was established back in the 1920s by the Russian psychologist Lev Vygotsky (Berk, 2000). He showed that young children can learn from a social group – they did not need any formal teaching to discover something. Vygotsky came up with the concept of what he called the "Zone of Proximal Development" (ZPD). Essentially, this is the gap between what you know as an individual and what you are capable of understanding as the next step. In order to progress your learning, you only need someone in your social group who knows a little bit more than you to help you get to that slightly higher level of understanding. All they need to do is provide what Vygotsky called "scaffolding" – tiny pieces of support – to help you gain the additional knowledge. There is inevitably someone who knows a little more about one thing within any informal student group than another student. They can help with scaffolding to move the other student along their ZPD to a state of higher knowledge. This is why students find informal study groups so valuable. They help them increase their knowledge and understanding without it seeming tough because they are supported by their peers who only know a little more than them. That doesn't seem as intimidating as asking a professor ...!

However, when studying online, there is no opportunity to learn almost randomly from other students. You will not meet them in the coffee bars or bump into them in the corridor. This is where online forums can be so valuable. Many students who study online ignore the forums and discussion groups. Yet, they can make a significant difference by providing the ideas and support that would typically be found in informal face-to-face study groups. So, make sure you take advantage of the forums and discussion groups.

> **QUICK TIP:** *Find out about all the forums and discussion groups for your courses and sign up to take part. Ignoring these forums could lower your chances of success.*

▶ ACADEMIC DISCUSSION GROUPS USED BY ONLINE STUDENTS

There are several different kinds of discussion groups used in on-line study. They are not always called "discussion groups", so it is worthwhile finding out the variety of names that may be used. These can include:

- Chat
- Chat room
- Discussion group
- Forum
- Newsgroup
- Room
- Team
- Wiki.

There may also be names for discussion groups peculiar to your university or specific to the software you are asked to use. You won't always be using something called "discussion" or "forum" to have group chats. There will also be different forums for different purposes. For instance, in one of the modules that I teach, there are the following discussion forums:

- **Welcome forum** – a discussion group that is there only for the first couple of weeks, enabling students to get to know one another. It is informal and has nothing academic contained within it.
- **Module forum** – this forum is where academic discussions occur and where students can ask questions about anything to do with the module.

- **Study group forum** – this is for the students to chat about anything they like related to the module. There is no academic input from me, though I may answer questions.
- **Tutorial forum** – a discussion group for each of the weekly tutorial sessions.

These forums replicate what tends to happen in the informal group discussions that students would have on a traditional campus. They would have informal groupings, and they would also meet up to discuss tutorial work, for instance. However, there may be other forums that do not replace typical student discussions. For example, I have forums that are there specifically for students to contribute to a discussion which is then assessed according to the level of involvement made by each individual student. Other forums also exist for online students, which does not happen with traditional face-to-face teaching.

Formal class forums

When you are studying online, you are likely to have at least one formal class forum for every module you attend. These forums provide support from the module leader as well as additional information to help you with your studies of that particular subject.

Some of these forums do not lead to much discussion. They are merely a means of communicating important information. For example, in my modules, I have a standard discussion forum called "Announcements". It is where I provide important information to students on the topics we are covering each week, as well as other details they need to know. Sometimes students respond to say thank you or to ask a question for clarification, but mostly these forums are one way – me providing information to the students.

Other formal class forums do require you to take part. One kind of formal forum where your participation is essential is in a discussion that is a component of your assessment. Lecturers will use such forums in two ways. Either you can use the discussion as a means of self-assessment so that you can check your progress. Or the forum would be used as a means of assessing your knowledge and understanding, instead of you having to write an essay. Research has shown that when forums are used to help assess understanding, they can help improve a student's critical thinking (Yang, Newby, and Bill, 2005). In one of the forums that I use for class assessment, all the students get a series of questions in advance, and they answer these in the discussion. They are also expected to comment on the answers from other students. From what students have written, I can see how well they understand the topic and allocate marks accordingly. One of the forums that I use makes up 25 per cent of the marks for the entire module.

Other class forums and discussion groups are not assessed. These forums are general discussion areas for each week's class. They tend to provide further information and allow students to ask questions relating to the lectures or reading materials. They are designed to help you extend your learning. They are a replacement for the questions and discussions you might have in face-to-face lectures and classes. When lectures are given in traditional campus universities, students will sometimes interrupt and ask for clarification. Or they may seek out the lecturer at the end of the session and ask questions or discuss a point. Sometimes, students will go and visit the lecturer in their office to talk about some aspect of the lecture. Clearly, none of this happens with online learning. Hence, these general class forums provide an alternative method of asking questions and gaining clarification. Your lecturer will answer, but so can other students. Indeed, that is an added bonus of online forums like this, which is not usually possible in face-to-face classes. In that situation, even if a student knows the answer, everyone is waiting for the lecturer to respond. When a question is asked in an online forum, another student can often respond before the lecturer checks in and sees the question. This means that general discussion forums provide a means of peer learning. Learning from other students in this way has been shown to help individuals develop their cognitive skills (Topping et al., 2017). Consequently it is a good idea to take part in these forums.

There is another reason why you should participate, and that is it contributes to the knowledge that your lecturers have about you. If they can see that you are participating and contributing well, the lecturer for that module will know that you are coping with your studies. However, if you don't participate, the module leader will have no way of knowing how you are getting on until your final assessments – and by then it is too late to do anything about it. If I see a student is not contributing to the forums, I can ask them why that is the case. I could also talk to their Personal Tutor about the lack of participation so that they could discuss it with the student informally. Also, if you participate and get things wrong, then the lecturer can help clarify things for you. If the only place you show a lack of understanding is in the exam, it is too late ...! Participating in general class forums is therefore of real help to you. It enables increased learning, and it assists you in putting things right before assessments take place.

> **QUICK TIP:** *Take part in formal class forums even if you think you will make a mistake or ask a silly question. It is a safe area to improve your knowledge and understanding, and in doing so, you'll be able to avoid losing marks in your assignments.*

Informal topic forums

Sometimes you will find that lecturers add informal forums to discuss the topic generally, without linking them to anything specific in the lectures. These forums are also used to allow students to chat with one another and even have a bit of fun with their learning. Generally, you will find that lecturers do not get involved with such forums. These discussion groups are seen mainly as a student place. In a sense, they are a replacement for discussing things with your mates in the coffee shop or in the bar, with the proviso that the discussion is about the subject being studied. These forums are worth popping into every now and then to see what is happening and to avoid missing out on helpful information. They also help build a rapport with other students.

Other academic forums

In addition to the forums for each of the subjects being studied, you will also find several other formal forums where you can ask questions or take part in discussions. These could include forums related to:

- Academic integrity and plagiarism
- Academic skills
- Assessments and exams
- Referencing
- The library.

Each of these will include important information, and there may well be answers to questions that you have thought about. So, it is vital to keep an eye on these general academic forums too. Otherwise, you could miss out on vital information that will make your studies easier or that will help you gain marks. All too often, students ignore these broader forums, and that is a shame because they are often packed with informative posts and discussion points.

> QUICK TIP: Keep an eye on all the academic forums so that you can see new and relevant information to help you with your studies.

▶ STUDENT-ONLY DISCUSSION GROUPS

Some universities provide forums for students to discuss all kinds of aspects of their studies and university life. These forums are self-moderated by the student groups involved, and there is no academic input. Such forums and chat rooms are sometimes also run by the Student Union. There will be forums for clubs, societies, sports groups, and so on. In addition, there will be discussions relating to studying, places to have a moan, and even forums where you might find love as they are used just to socialise.

In some cases, there are dozens of forums available to you, and it is all too easy to get carried away checking out all the discussions on a wide variety of topics. Indeed, you are more likely to be distracted in this way than you would be in the "real world" on campus. That's because if you were studying at a traditional university, you would have to seek out all the discussions going on. You would need to go to the meetings, for example, of a club or society to take part in any debates. However, when the forums are all online, you can dip in and out quickly without having to go further than your armchair. As a result, you need to be disciplined in your use of informal discussion groups as you could become somewhat distracted, taking your mind off your studies and eating into your available time. Detailed advice on dealing with distractions can be found in Chapter 10.

Social media discussion groups

Many students set up informal groups on social media. There may also be pre-existing study groups on social networks such as Facebook. Also, reasonably near the start of each module, at least one student will set up a WhatsApp group to start chatting about the lectures and the work that needs doing. These social groups can be beneficial for students. Not only do they provide you with ideas and information about your studies, but these social networking groups have another critical function for distance learning students. These social media groups will provide you with a sense of belonging and being part of the community of students. If you were studying at a traditional university, you would get that sense of belonging simply by wandering around the campus. Indeed, recently I had to go back to my old university, the University of

Surrey, where I completed my first degree. I'd been asked to give a talk at a meeting in the Business School there, and as soon as I arrived on campus after many years away, I immediately felt "at home". That sense of belonging that I had for my three years of undergraduate study was still with me such a long time afterwards. There is a saying in academic circles, "You might leave the university, but the university never leaves you". That sense of belonging is much easier to feel when it is associated with a location. However, many students who study online will only have their bedroom or the local coffee shop as the place they associate with their degree. Their sense of belonging will be much reduced compared with traditional university students. That's why student social media groups can be so important to distance learning students. These discussion groups can help you become part of a community and give you that feeling of belonging. Even if you are not a fan of social media and try to avoid it as much as possible, taking part in the student groups on networks such as Facebook or LinkedIn can be helpful in making you "feel like a proper student". In fact, there is research that shows that students who do take part in social media discussion groups enhance their use of the formal forums within the module itself (Kent, 2016).

> QUICK TIP: *Join relevant social networking groups for your university and your degree studies. Even if you are only an occasional user, they give you a sense of belonging and can boost your studies.*

▶ STUDY WIKIS

Wikis are collaboratively produced sets of web pages. The first wiki was established in 1995. The developer of the first online wiki was a programmer who wanted to create sets of web pages quickly. Rather than call it something like "quick web", he coined the term "wiki", which is derived from the Hawaiian word *wiki-wiki*, which means "fast" or "quick" (Leuf and Cunningham, 2001).

Many online modules will include a wiki, and I mention them here because they are places where you can discuss information. Often a wiki has a discussion section akin to a forum, as well as the main wiki pages themselves.

You may find wikis embedded within your module materials. Popular VLE software, such as Blackboard and Moodle, contain wiki tools. These will be set up by the module leader or course administrator. They are available for students to compile shared notes, for example, and discuss what they are learning. Other popular academic software, such as Canvas or Google Classroom, do not contain wikis, as such. In Canvas, you would just be editing a page, and in Google Classroom, you would be working on a shared Google Doc document. Some universities now use Microsoft Teams to run online learning environments, and this includes a wiki option within each of the individual teams. Another possibility is that your module may include a Microsoft OneNote "class notebook". This is similar to the concept of a wiki in that anyone can edit the pages and add information collaboratively.

Regardless of the software used for your course wikis, they can be an essential part of your studies. Indeed, some lecturers will use the wikis as part of the assessments they make. You may also find that wikis are used for a tutorial group where everyone in the group collaborates to discuss a topic before the tutorial session.

However, despite their popularity, wikis as a means of discussion have some downsides that you will need to think about. The main problem that wikis have is the concept behind them, of needing to be able to collaborate fast. This means that in many instances, all you have is a blank page or a page with some text to which you can add extra material. It is usually just click and type. Often there are no stylistic tools, and making something bold, for instance, can be cumbersome compared with a word processor. This makes wikis unappealing for many people. Indeed, when comparing the use of wikis and forums for online studying, researchers found that wikis were not as popular (Kear et al., 2010). Indeed, students were somewhat concerned about wikis because they allow other students' contributions to be altered or even deleted. That's not possible with forums, chats, or discussion groups where everyone can see everyone's individual contribution. On a wiki, it is possible to alter or remove the contribution of others, and so this can lead to reluctance to use wikis because someone's work could be changed, or others would not know the originator of the material.

If your module leader requires you to use a wiki, especially if it will form part of your assessment, then it is crucial to get to know how you should edit wikis and be able to contribute. Read the help files for the particular software you are using, or check out the video links on the website I have created to accompany this book, https://studyingonline.tips. It would also be a good idea to ensure you know the rules or etiquette for using your university wiki so that you don't make mistakes. It's not necessarily as straightforward as you might think. Wikipedia, the world's most extensive wiki, has 26 "principles of etiquette" in addition to a range of other

TABLE 5.1 Differences between formatting text in a word processor and in a wiki

To make something bold in a word processor	To make something bold in a wiki
Highlight the word and select "Bold" or type Ctrl + B	Insert three single quotation marks before the word and three single quotation marks after the word
To indent something in a word processor	**To indent something in a wiki**
Hit the indent button on the menu or press tab	Type two colons before the indented material
To insert a table in a word processor	**To insert a table in a wiki**
Choose the menu option for tables and insert	Type an open bracket first. Then type the "pipe" symbol – I. Then add a dash for a row and add a pipe for each column. Then add a close bracket to end the table

elements of advice on how to stick to the guidelines for using the wiki (Wikipedia, 2021). That's in addition to a page full of individual policies and a further page of various guidelines. Using a wiki requires consideration for others in a more extensive way than a traditional forum or discussion group. This is because you will be directly editing and changing someone else's work, rather than just commenting upon it in a forum setting.

> **QUICK TIP:** *If your course uses wikis, make sure you understand how to use the software and the principles of usage. Otherwise, you could easily upset people.*

▶ PUBLIC DISCUSSION FORUMS

In addition to the forums and discussion groups provided by the university and your fellow students, there will inevitably be subject-based forums available across the Internet. For example, for one of the subjects that I teach – consumer behaviour – there are more than 140 discussion groups just on LinkedIn that students could join. There will, of course, be many more on other social networks as well as on a variety of websites. There will be no shortage of forums you could join for each of the subjects you are studying.

However, public discussion forums can present students with several difficulties, quite apart from the potential for distraction. The first problem is that in many instances these forums and discussion groups will not be providing information that is verified or that is based on evidence. They can often be full of opinions masquerading as fact. In the academic forums on your module websites, your lecturers will be taking care to present information that is evidence-based or which can be verified using reliable sources. In external discussion forums, you may be presented with information that sounds logical but is factually incorrect. Another issue with public forums is that the discussion may not be at the critical thinking level required for academic study. This will be of particular concern to Master's students.

However, public discussion forums can be of benefit to students. Often they present current thinking and ideas about a topic. This is different from textbooks which by their very nature are bound to be a year or so out-of-date, at best. Also, public discussion forums will often have experts in a particular field who could provide you with helpful information when doing your research for assignments, for example. Indeed, if you are struggling with your learning, then asking questions on public sites such as Quora or Reddit can provide you with some expert information at times and could be worth exploring because of this. In fact, if you ask a question on something like Quora, you may well find that lecturers from other universities are the individuals providing you with answers.

▶ HOW STUDENTS USE FORUMS

Students are like anyone else – they vary in their behaviour patterns and individual preferences for online activities. That means there is a wide variety of usage patterns when it comes to online forums. However, my anecdotal experience of working with students on forums over the past 20 years suggests there are three types of behaviour.

1. Avid use of the forum, making regular contributions
2. Lurking, only viewing and making no contributions
3. Ignoring the forum until forced to do so.

If I look back at the forums I have used over the last few years, I can see that the majority of the contributions come from a handful of students in each study group. However, I can also see several other students who log in regularly, read the materials on the forum, but never add anything themselves – not even a comment saying thank you. One thing I have also noticed is that the students who are avid users and who play a full part in the forum discussions are the ones who tend to get the highest marks.

> **QUICK TIP:** *If you want high marks, play an active role in the forums.*

Many students prefer to be "lurkers", just visiting the forum, reading what is there, and never taking an active part. One of the possible reasons for this is that the forums can seem isolated from classes. According to one study of the use of online forums by students, students appreciate it when the online discussions are extended into lecture classes (Hirschel, 2012). If you are taking hybrid classes with some online and some face-to-face sessions, the lecturer may integrate the forum discussions with information in class. However, with recorded online lectures, that is not always possible. Hence, one idea that you could use is to ask questions based on what was on the forum in any live online lectures or one-to-one sessions with lecturers. That way, you will benefit from extending the forum discussion, which appears to help integrate the ideas. Even if you are a lurker, you can do this.

▶ AVOIDING FEELING STUPID

One of the reasons why students do not take part in forums is they do not wish to appear stupid. They don't want to ask questions or make comments that make them seem like they do not understand. When I encourage students to participate in forums, I am often asked, "What if I say something that others will think is stupid? I don't want to appear as though I don't understand". I try to explain that even the world's top experts in a subject did not understand it, to begin with. Indeed, they only got to be those experts because they asked questions without worrying about what other people thought. Of course, that is easy for me to say, but it does not eliminate the feeling of inadequacy that many students have when being asked to contribute to a forum. Indeed, researchers in Norway and the Netherlands have found that the inhibition to take part in online forums is experienced by almost everyone (Sakariassen and Meijer, 2021). According to this research, there is a complex array of psychological reasons for non-participation. However, at the heart of our unwillingness to take part is worrying about what people might think of us. The study also demonstrated that our self-identity is at risk if we take part in online discussions. This would suggest that people who don't worry about what other people think of them and who are comfortable with their own identity are going to be the ones who take part fully in forums. You might not fall into the category of those comfortable people, so what can you do about it?

One possible answer is to take part in a small way so that you can see that there is a positive reaction to your participation. This will reassure you that you are doing the right thing, and your self-identity will therefore not be tarnished. You could, for example, try small comments with follow-up questions. For instance, if someone has made a reasonable contribution, you could say:

> "That's interesting. Could you expand on it a little? I'd be interested to know more".

You will then get a reply providing more information. You may also get other people saying that they would also appreciate the additional material. The result of this is a little boost to your confidence and increased comfort with taking part in the discussion forum.

Sometimes you will find that you are forced to take part in forums. They may form the basis for tutorials, for instance, where you will extend the discussion in a video conference call. At other times your participation will be compulsory because you are being assessed. Even so, you may still feel inhibited and somewhat shy. Again, tentative steps at first, contributing small comments will build your confidence and allow you to take a more active part later on. However, this means ensuring you know the timetable.

It is no good trying to take those baby steps in forum participation if there is only a day or two left before the forum closes for the assessment or before a tutorial. You need to ensure you start taking part from the beginning. Otherwise, you will not be able to contribute as you would like, which could lead to a loss of marks if the forum is assessed.

▶ PLANNED PARTICIPATION IN FORUMS

One way to help ensure your participation is to plan it and schedule it within your timetable. All too often, students do not get the best out of the available online forums because they forget about them. They are told to visit the forum at the start of a module, for instance, and then do not return unless they are reminded. That also means students do not participate. Every now and then, they look when someone reminds them, but they do not feel part of the discussion and hence observe rather than contribute. This issue can be avoided if you check in to the forum regularly. Create a timeslot for checking in to the forums in your calendar. Indeed, if you make it a routine, you will find it is easier to participate.

If you have a routine for checking in every day at 3:00 pm, for example, it becomes a habit. This means you do not have to think about it. Nor do you have to worry about whether you have contributed because you will know. The regular routine will also help increase your number of contributions. That has a double impact. First, you reduce the anxiety about taking part because you will have done it so many times. Second, you will almost certainly increase your marks for the module because higher participation rates are associated with good marks.

> QUICK TIP: Set a routine in your calendar for regular forum participation.

▶ SUBSCRIBING TO FORUMS

Many forums will have subscription options. The software will let you tick a box or click on a link to "subscribe". This will add you to a mailing list that sends out notifications of forum posts to your email inbox. When you subscribe, it means that you avoid missing out on what is taking place in the forum. However, you can also get annoyed by all the repetitive email messages which merely tell you about a forum post that says "Thank you" when someone responds to a comment, for example.

One way out of this is to create a filter in your email system. If you are unsure how to do this, check out the help files for your particular email program. For example, popular email programs such as Apple Mail, Gmail, and Microsoft Outlook all provide methods of filtering emails. You could set up a filter to divert all the emails from the forum subscription service into a specific mail folder. You would then only check that folder when you wanted to, perhaps on a daily basis. This would avoid you being constantly interrupted but would also mean that you were always aware of what was happening in the forum.

An alternative to this is to use RSS feeds. RSS stands for "Really Simple Syndication", though, frankly, it is only "really simple" for computer engineers ...! For the rest of us, it is just a method of collecting information from a variety of sources. Many forums produce an RSS feed. This provides you with the entire output of the forum, which is automatically updated each time something new is added. The way to make this work is to get an RSS Reader program. Popular ones include Feedly or Feedspot, which both have free options.

To use these RSS readers, you add the RSS feed from your forum as a subscription to your chosen reader program. In Feedly, for instance, you just press the button saying "Create new feed". Then you enter the address of your RSS feed from the forum (just copy and paste). The RSS reader then collects the information from the

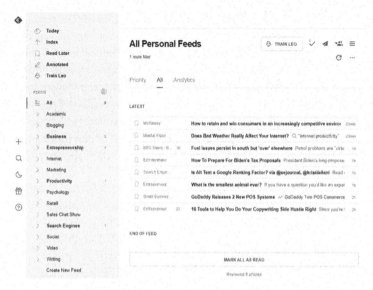

Figure 5.1 An RSS reader can collect together a range of sources of information, including forum posts

forum and displays new posts for you. Doing this means you can arrange to have all the forums you subscribe to in one place, without the need for interruptions through email. On my computer, I have set up Feedly as a pinned tab in my web browser. This means that at regular intervals during the day, I can go to that tab and check to see the latest information from a variety of sources. This saves a great deal of time. Plus, it means I am in control of the receipt of that information. You could do the same, meaning that you would have a single place to check the forums you need to monitor.

PRACTICAL TIPS

- **Check out all the forums available to you.** Search through your online VLE to find all the tutorials and discussion groups available. If you don't find everything that is available, you could miss out.

- **Take part in academic forums.** Even if you think you will make mistakes or appear stupid, it is worthwhile taking part in academic forums. This is because you will learn and correct any errors in understanding. You can do that before you come to any assessment. As a result, forums can help you avoid losing marks.
- **Join social media groups.** Even if you only take part occasionally, they can contribute to you feeling more part of a student community rather than an individual studying alone.
- **Ask questions on public forums.** Ask questions on public forums such as Quora as this can help increase your knowledge and understanding by gaining insights from experts outside your university.
- **Set up a forum routine.** Put regular slots in your timetable for taking part in forums. That way, you will not forget to take part, and the regularity of reading forums will help you gain confidence in participation.

▶ REFERENCES

Berk, L.E. (2000) *Child Development*, 5th edn. Boston, MA: Allyn and Bacon.

Bertram, C. (2004) '"Students Doing It for Themselves": The Role of Informal Study Groups in a Mixed Mode Teacher Education Programme', *South African Journal of Higher Education*, 17(2), pp. 218–225.

Hirschel, R. (2012) 'Moodle: Students' Perspectives on Forums, Glossaries and Quizzes', *The JALT CALL Journal*, 74(8), pp. 95–112.

Kear, K., Woodthorpe, J., Robertson, S. and Hutchison, M. (2010) 'From Forums to Wikis: Perspectives on Tools for Collaboration', *The Internet and Higher Education*, 13(4), pp. 218–225.

Kent, M. (2016) 'Adding to the Mix: Students Use of Facebook Groups and Blackboard Discussion Forums in Higher Education', *Knowledge Management & E-Learning*, 8(3), pp. 444–463.

Leuf, B. and Cunningham, W. (2001) *The Wiki Way: Quick Collaboration on the Web*. Boston, MA: Addison-Wesley.

Sakariassen, H. and Meijer, I.C. (2021) 'Why so Quiet? Exploring Inhibition in Digital Public Spaces', *European Journal of Communication*, p. 02673231211017346.

Topping, K., Buchs, C., Duran, D. and van Keer, H. (2017) *Effective Peer Learning*. Abingdon: Routledge.

Wikipedia (2021) 'Etiquette'. Wikipedia. Available at: https://en.wikipe
dia.org/wiki/Wikipedia:Etiquette (Accessed: 26 September 2021).
Yang, Y.-T.C., Newby, T.J. and Bill, R.L. (2005) 'Using Socratic Ques-
tioning to Promote Critical Thinking Skills through Asynchronous
Discussion Forums in Distance Learning Environments', *American
Journal of Distance Education*, 19(3), pp. 163–181.

6 Using video

There is little doubt that it is the availability of web-based video that has been the trigger for so much online teaching. Online video has been technically available since the mid-1990s. One of the first websites to host video was called Newgrounds, which was launched in 1995. However, at that time, few people had sufficient bandwidth to watch video, and speeds were very low. It wasn't until broadband started to expand in 2005 that it was possible for many people to watch online video. That was the year that saw the birth of YouTube in San Francisco when three ex-PayPal employees got together to start the service, which they sold to Google a year or so later. However, it wasn't until 2014 that online video really took off when a new encoding format known as HTML5 became widespread. Before that, for instance, "live streaming" was complex and cumbersome. It also meant that video conferencing often required specialist equipment and costly services to manage the vast amounts of data. With HTML5, increased broadband speeds, and the ability to run video live within web pages, it finally became possible for almost anyone to create high-quality video presentations. It also meant that web-based video conferencing became possible. These two advances together made online education feasible. However, the relatively recent availability of online

DOI: 10.4324/9781003259695-8

video services means that studying online using video is recent history. That's why a great deal of online video for education is still somewhat experimental. You will see lecturers trying out new ideas and some failing to succeed. That's because it is so new to education. After all, universities have been around since the eleventh century: the first university was founded in 1088 in Bologna, Italy. That's over 900 years of teaching, but online video teaching only having been available for less than a decade.

The novelty of online video teaching is visible to all students. Some of the videos you watch will be highly professional, with lecturers who are comfortable being TV presenters. However, you will also discover video lectures that are poorly presented with presentation techniques that are sadly lacking. Most lecturers have years of experience in a lecture theatre and have learned what to do by observing their own lecturers doing the same thing when they were at university. Nowadays, though, with online video, there is a significant lack of experience due to its relatively recent introduction. As a result, when studying online, you will face some brilliant material and some inadequate lectures, to say the least.

It somewhat reminds me of an event several years ago at the University of Cambridge. I had helped organise a conference for doctors which was held in the Peterhouse Theatre, one of the oldest lecture theatres in what is the oldest Cambridge college. The place was steeped in history. We had organised every last piece of technology you could imagine for all of the guest speakers. However, one of the speakers – a Cambridge professor and Nobel Prize winner – had not notified us of the presentational equipment he would require. As far as we, the organisers, were concerned, we had everything. This professor was to give the opening keynote address. At the time the conference was scheduled to begin, he had not shown up. I was frantically trying to find him and suggesting to the conference chairman how he might "fill" until we could track down the prof. As people were settling into their seats, a door at the back of the stage opened and in walked our keynote speaker. He had a pile of papers in his hand and shuffled across to the podium where he placed all his notes. Then he looked around at all the technology provided and asked, "Is there a blackboard

I can use?" He went on to deliver a stunning speech without any visual aids because the one piece of technology I had not thought of getting for the conference was a blackboard.

This story indicates how lecturers love to use the somewhat old-fashioned ways of delivery. Indeed, only recently I was involved in moving offices at my university. We had established a new faculty by combining some schools of study, which meant some people had to move to a different building on campus. It was during this move that I discovered one of my colleagues had an overhead projector. I thought they were ancient history, but clearly, someone doesn't agree with me. If you don't know what an overhead projector is, it is a device where you place a transparent sheet on top of a glass panel and write on it. The panel has a bright bulb that shines what you have written up towards a mirror to project it onto a white screen.

The fact that one professor I met loves blackboards and another colleague clearly uses an overhead projector is an indication that old technology has not entirely gone away. Many lecturers have decades of experience and background in teaching with these old technologies, and change is uncomfortable for them. That's why you will see examples of video lectures that are not as good as you would expect. It is because lecturers are being torn away from their beloved ways of doing things into a new, modern world.

Of course, despite some poor videos, there are also many excellent online videos for you to watch, with many lecturers becoming adept at using this new way of teaching. Even so, you need to be prepared for the fact that not all online video is of an Oscar-winning standard. There is a great deal of varied output you will encounter as an online student. It is good to be prepared for this.

> QUICK TIP: If you do have to watch an online lecture of poor quality, do a quick search on YouTube for the same topic, and you may well find a better alternative.

▶ THE USES OF ONLINE VIDEO

You will be using online video in a variety of ways when you are studying online. Lectures are an obvious use for video. You will be asked to watch recorded lectures regularly. However, there are many other uses for online video within education. For instance, not all lectures will be recorded. Some will be delivered live using online video conferencing software. Other lectures will be provided in a "webinar" format. Also, different lecturers will take varied approaches to how they create online lectures. Some, for instance, will use what is known as "lecture capture". Essentially, this is a camera in a traditional lecture theatre that follows the lecturer around as they talk and shows any slides they use simultaneously. Some recorded lectures will be in this form. The lecturer will deliver the talk in an empty lecture theatre and use the capture system to record it. Other lecturers will sit at their computers and record the lecture on a webcam. Yet other lecturers will go to a campus studio and record their lectures there so they appear more professional. You will also find lectures vary in length - some last an hour or two, but you may get lectures that last just a few minutes. Personally, my video recordings tend to be around five to ten minutes. I break down a 90-minute lecture, for instance, into a series of short video presentations. That way, I hope to maintain the interest of the students watching.

Another use of online video is for tutorial sessions or seminars. Generally, these will be held live using web conferencing software such as Adobe Connect, Microsoft Teams, or Zoom. The tutorial leader, who may be your lecturer or perhaps one of their PhD students, may show some slides using screen share, or they may ask you to download some files presented in the "chat" stream. You will then be expected to participate in discussions or ask questions using your webcam.

Video is also used by online students in group work. When you are studying at a distance, group work needs careful coordination. Many students find that Zoom calls or video chats through

Microsoft Teams are helpful in organising the work and sharing the workload. Group work is increasingly common in undergraduate study as it helps prepare students for the workplace. As a result, you are likely to be using online video regularly for the group work activities you are required to do. For example, you may need to work as a group in preparation for a seminar. Or you may need to prepare joint work for a group assignment, and organising that via a video call would be helpful.

A further use of online video is in assessment. You could be required to record video presentations for an assignment, for example. Poster presentations are a common means of assessment as well, and presenting these at a distance to the university is only feasible using online video. So, it is not only lecturers who will have to get used to using this relatively new educational technology. As a student, you too are going to need to get to grips with creating videos.

▶ THE BENEFITS OF ONLINE VIDEO

Video has obvious benefits. You can see your lecturer, for instance, in a recorded lecture. You can also see your fellow students in an online tutorial. If you couldn't see the faces of the people involved in your classes, you would find it much less engaging and, therefore, more challenging to complete your online studies.

Even so, many students are reluctant to use video. They are happy to watch the video of the lectures but much more reluctant to switch on their webcam. Since the Covid pandemic started at the beginning of 2020, I have run online tutorial sessions on Microsoft Teams. However, after running over 300 tutorials online, I have yet to participate in one where every student switched on their webcams. Indeed, I have run many tutorials where I was the only person who had their camera on. Reasons given (or should that be excuses) included "poor Internet", "there are other people in the house", and even "I haven't brushed my hair yet". The "poor

Internet" is often blatantly untrue because students who complain about "lack of bandwidth" are only too ready to talk about what they are watching on TV streaming services like Netflix. If they really had a poor Internet connection, they wouldn't be able to watch subscription television. Instead, the students are providing what seems a logical reason to cover their reluctance to use video. This suggests that the students are not convinced of the benefits of having their cameras switched on during video conference calls.

I have discussed this lack of desire to switch on the webcam with several students and discovered that one of the critical factors involved is self-identity. That relates to the same issues discussed in Chapter 5 about the unwillingness to participate in online forums. How we perceive ourselves and what we believe others will think about us is central to the reluctance to use webcams. Mistakenly, students think that people will be critical of their appearance, for instance. Yet, those same students would not worry about this in a face-to-face session on campus. The reason is that on campus you cannot see yourself. On online video conference calls, you are shown your own image on screen together with everyone else. That means we are constantly aware of what we look like, and this triggers concerns. So, the best way out of that, seemingly, is to switch off the webcam so we cannot see ourselves. However, the problem with doing that is that you remove the benefit of other students seeing you and engaging more with you as an individual. In face-to-face sessions on campus, you would be visible to others in the group in a tutorial, for instance. Without your webcam switched on, you disappear from the view of the others on a video conference, and so you are more likely to be ignored.

Check out the software that your university uses for video conference calls. Some software allows you to switch off seeing yourself. If that is not the case, you can get a sticky note and place it on the screen where your image is to cover yourself. That way, you will not be aware of seeing yourself, thereby reducing that anxiety and increasing your overall engagement and benefit from using online video.

QUICK TIP: *If you don't want to see yourself in an online video call, open up the app on Windows called Sticky Notes and place a new note over the area of the screen that has your image.*

Engagement with others is a clear benefit of using online video. Another critical reason for using online video is that it helps you learn. The cognitive theory of multimedia learning was developed by Professor Richard E. Mayer from the University of California (Mayer, 2009). This theory suggests that we only have two "channels" for decoding information. One channel is auditory, and one is visual. Each of these channels is thought to have a finite capacity, so we have to "offload" information from each channel into memory to create a representation of what we are studying. Professor Mayer's work shows that this construction of a representation of the information we are studying is more accessible when we have words and pictures together rather than words alone. In other words, when we add video to support the delivery of information, it is easier for your brain to construct representations of what is going on. Without images or video, it is more demanding for your brain. Figure 6.1 summarises this.

The multimedia benefit of video could help explain why students find online video learning so valuable. Indeed, evidence shows that students who engage well with online video materials gain higher marks than students who do not use these videos (Carmichael,

Figure 6.1 Words alone are more challenging to understand than words with pictures

Reid, and Karpicke, 2018). There appears to be a consistent gain in marks by a few percentage points when students use online videos. Even though this might seem only a tiny amount, the few points could mean the difference between one grade boundary or another, meaning you could get a higher class of degree simply by engaging with the videos.

> **QUICK TIP:** *Watch all the lecture videos and other videos on your module. The multimedia approach means you will learn more, and this is linked to higher marks.*

You might think, though, that the only benefit of videos comes from those that have high production values and which present a rich and diverse array of material. Students sometimes look at a lecture video and realise it is one of those from a lecturer uncomfortable with the new technology who has produced a rather dry video that is not exciting to watch. However, avoiding such videos is not a good idea. Research has shown that the diversity of media is not related to student outcomes (Costley and Lange, 2017). The variety of material presented to students doesn't appear to matter a great deal. What does seem to be of greater relevance is that the video comes from lecturers at the student's own university (Carmichael et al., 2018). This is more evidence that regardless of the basic nature of some videos you will be asked to watch, viewing them will help your studies. So, get watching ...!

▶ WATCH LECTURES ONLINE WITH ANOTHER STUDENT

If you were studying on campus, you would be going to lectures with other students. The lecture would then be a shared experience. However, for many students who study at a distance online, watching recorded lectures is a solitary experience. This means you do not get the same experience as students who visit lecture theatres together. They will chat about the lecture as they sit next to each other. They will chat about the lecture with one another over lunch. It's rather like going to the cinema. People tend to do that with someone else. They share the experience together and talk about it afterwards. Watching online lectures on your own can be tedious because you realise you are doing it alone and have no one to chat to about what you watched. Researchers in Canada investigated whether watching online videos whilst remotely connected to someone else was beneficial (Macaranas et al., 2013). It turned out that people were more engaged with the video they watched if they were also connected by video to someone else at the same time. You could do this, for instance, by watching the video on your laptop whilst being in a video call with a fellow student on your mobile phone. This is not as daft as it sounds. In a recent conversation with students, I discovered that a small group of them would even read textbooks and do their online research while in an ongoing video conference call with each other. They told me that often very little was said. They would start the call, have a quick check-in style chat with each other and then get on with their work. They kept the call open so they could see each other in the corner of their screen. But, otherwise, they just carried on with their work, occasionally chatting or asking each other questions. When I asked why they did this, they told me it helped them engage with the module materials more. The fact that they could see others were studying motivated them to work as well. This should not be that surprising. As I walk around campus each day, I see groups of students sitting together but studying independently. They are reading books or making notes while sitting with fellow students. This togetherness appears to help. It improves engagement with materials and increases motivation. But, as someone studying online, you miss out on this unless you arrange to engage with module materials while in a video call with fellow students.

QUICK TIP: *Form a video study group so that you can call each other on your phones and then watch an online video at the same time on your laptops. This joint viewing will improve your engagement with the recordings you watch.*

▶ GET A GOOD WEBCAM

When you are studying at a distance online, you will be expected to participate in online tutorials, seminars, and workshops. You will need a good camera if you are to make the most of your years as an online student. Most laptops come with a built-in camera these days. This makes them convenient as you do not need additional equipment. However, the webcams built into the edge of a laptop screen are not always high quality. This results in a poor image of you for the other people taking part in the online sessions. This may not seem to be of great importance. After all, they can see you, just not clearly. Imagine, though, you were in a face-to-face class on campus, and you could not see the other people in the room clearly. You would find it challenging to engage with them. The same is true online. If people cannot see each other clearly, it is more difficult to work with them. Indeed, in a study that included a comparison of laptop webcam use with high definition (HD) cameras in video calls, people found the laptop cameras did not give them a good sense of sharing a space with other individuals (Aaltonen et al., 2009). This suggests that low-quality webcam use makes people feel more distant from one another. That is not going to be good for you or your fellow students if you are going to be doing a large number of online video calls during the 2–4 years of your degree. As outlined in Chapter 2, you really need a separate webcam, regardless of what your laptop provides. A high-quality webcam will improve your visibility for other students. It will also reduce the lag between your contribution and when other people see your input. Plus, good webcams have much better sync between image and sound.

> **QUICK TIP:** *Even if your laptop has an inbuilt camera, get an external HD webcam as it will improve your online study experience.*

There is a seemingly endless array of webcams available and a similarly never-ending supply of blog posts and articles advising you about the latest "best buys". However, there are some fundamentals that you can apply to making that purchasing decision. You need to consider the factors listed below when buying a webcam.

Resolution

The camera's resolution determines how many pixels (individual components of the image) can be captured by the webcam. It might seem logical to go for the highest resolution you can get. However, this can cause problems. The more pixels that are captured, the more data has to be transmitted across the Internet. This can slow things down and eat into your bandwidth. As an example, look at Figure 6.2. A high-quality HD camera only has to transmit around one-quarter of the number of pixels compared with the next highest level of image quality. So, an HD camera is ideal for online video calls. However, if you are going to record material, such as for assessed presentations, then a UHD 4K camera would be better as the image quality is more than double that of HD. Rather than getting two cameras, look for webcams that can vary the resolution. Some of the leading cameras come with software that allows you to adjust the resolution depending upon the work you are doing.

Frame rate

The camera's frame rate is a measure of how many still images the camera produces per second. The more still images per second, the smoother your video will look. However, rather like

Camera type	Resolution	Total number of pixels
HD Ready	1280 x 720	921,600
Full HD	1920 x 1080	2,073,600
UHD (4K)	3840 x 2160	8,294,400

Figure 6.2 Resolutions and numbers of pixels for different webcams

resolution, the more frames per second (fps), the more data that needs transmitting. That can be a problem when you are involved in video conference calls. Many of the more expensive cameras provide software that allows you to adjust the frame rate. Ideally, get a camera that lets you change the frame rate depending on your activity. Streaming your webcam needs lower frame rates than recording videos.

Field of view

Another critical factor for students studying online, particularly if you are home, is the field of view. This is a representation of how much of your surroundings will be visible. The field of view is measured in angles which show the angle from the camera towards you. Many webcams have wide fields of view of 90 degrees. That means a large amount of your surroundings will be visible during the call. This may not be appropriate as you may have elements of your home that you do not want to be displayed to others. Equally, with a wide field of view, your face becomes proportionally smaller, making it tougher for the other participants to engage with you. Ideally, you need a webcam with a narrow field of view of 60 degrees.

Webcam fixing

There are many other features that the webcam manufacturers will want to promote. However, there is really only one other item that is crucial for you. This is how the webcam will be fixed. Many webcams come with attachments that allow them to be fixed to the top of a monitor. However, these can be too wide for use on thinner laptop screens. So, you will need to check to make sure that the fixing is appropriate for laptops. Alternatively, you could get a desktop tripod. Most webcams come with the option for them to be mounted on a tripod. You can get pretty cheap desktop tripods, and you could then put your webcam onto one of these and position it behind the screen of your laptop. This could be of real help because, in many instances, a webcam on a laptop screen can obscure the top of the monitor itself, making it more difficult for you to work. Hence, having the webcam on a separate tripod will avoid this issue for you.

▶ CHECK YOUR LIGHTING

The images your webcam captures will depend upon the lighting in your room. You will probably have been on video conference calls where you cannot see someone clearly. The reason for this could be their webcam quality, but frequently it is the level of lighting that is inadequate. If you watch the TV news, you will often notice that there is a wide shot of the entire studio as the programme begins, and you will see several massive lights in the roof space. Even though all that is happening is that the news-reader is doing just that, reading the news out to you, there is a significant amount of high-powered lighting. Even with the sophisticated broadcast cameras used by news corporations, lighting is still of fundamental importance. Many years ago, I had a job as a stage electrician at a theatre in Guildford, Surrey. My task was to help the lighting director ensure that the actors and performers could be seen clearly. That would often involve a dozen or more bright lights just focused on one part of the stage. Up in the fly loft above the stage, there would be hundreds of lights. Doing this job helped me understand the fundamental importance of lighting. Not only does it help the visibility of, in the case of theatres, actors, it is also crucial in creating the mood of the audience. When it comes to online video, the lighting of the participants will be important in ensuring visibility as well as creating moods. Sometimes the moods caused by the poor lighting may not be the ones the individual wants to be associat-ed with them. If your lighting is not good, your video conference calls could make people think differently about you as they sub-consciously associate a particular mood with you. That's before you even consider your visibility and the resulting engagement others will have with you. All too often, lighting for online video is never given a thought. Yet, just as in the case of TV or the theatre, lighting plays a fundamental role in how you will be perceived. So it is clearly worthwhile getting it right.

Selecting the right video lights

There are plenty of options for video lights, from the very cheap to the highly professional and super expensive. Unless you want to be an online video star, there is no need to spend a great deal of money. The aim of the lighting should be to illuminate your face so that the rest of the people on the video call can see you clearly. The standard way of doing this is to use something called a "three-point lighting setup". As shown in Figure 6.3, you have a "key light", which is aimed at your face and brightens your appearance. A second light facing you is known as the "fill light". This is on the other side of the key light but is aimed slightly lower. As its name suggests, this light fills in the shadows created by the key light. Finally, there is the "back light", which is placed behind

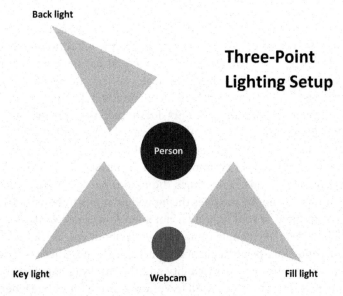

Figure 6.3 A typical three-point lighting setup

you, usually directly opposite the fill light. The back light creates a small area of light behind your head which then appears to separate you from the room's background. Together, these three lights will make you appear clearly on screen. If you don't have the space for a back light, then the two lights at the front will be sufficient. I only have two lights which cost me about £35. People often comment how well they can see me when I am on video calls. So, it doesn't cost much to stand out.

Another popular form of lighting these days is "ring lighting". These are, as the name suggests, rings of light. They are primarily designed to surround professional cameras rather than webcams. They are popular with online video influencers, for example. The ring light is placed around the lens of their professional camera, and when they look directly into that lens, their face becomes very well lit. Ring lights help avoid shadows when you are looking directly into the lens surrounded by the light. However, you are not likely to be able to place your webcam in the centre of the ring. Consequently you can't have the benefits of the ring light unless that the webcam is of a kind that allows you to place it in the ring light.

One other factor to consider is the use of filters. Many lights come with filters that allow you to reduce the hardness of the light. An unfiltered light provides a "hard" light that can wash out areas of your face and make your appearance somewhat unrealistic. Hence a "soft" light is better. These days, most video lighting kits come with filters that can soften the light or add colour effects. What you don't want for your lighting setup is an LED panel that has no means of softening the brightness. So, select lighting that has a filter over the lights themselves.

▶ CHECK WHAT'S BEHIND YOU

When you are on camera during tutorials, seminars, or other video conference calls, it is worthwhile remembering that people can see behind you. During the Covid pandemic, when many experts were interviewed via Skype or Zoom on television news programmes, there was the "battle of the bookcases". Every interviewee seemed to have an array of books behind them. This led to several social media memes about displaying books behind you on Zoom calls.

You do not need a bookcase behind you. However, you do need to ensure that the background is not distracting. Recently, I was running a tutorial where one student was sitting at a desk in her bedroom. Apart from the fact that the bed we could see behind her had not been made, it was covered with fluffy toy creatures. That might not have been the look that she wanted her fellow students to see. Also, it could be distracting to fellow students. Instead of listening to the discussion in the tutorial, they may have started wondering why their fellow student seemed to have a childish streak. Or they may have thought about the untidiness of her room. Either way, they would not be thinking about the content of the tutorial. So, if there were a set of rules about backgrounds, the first one would be to make the area behind you at least tidy ...!

> **QUICK TIP: Before you appear on any video conference call, make sure your room is tidy and presentable.**

It is also worthwhile remembering that online video conference calls may be recorded. Therefore whatever is in your background could be permanently available for others to see. A pinboard on the wall behind you with a sticky note showing your computer password is not a good idea. Yes, that has been seen as well. Make sure you are happy for that whatever is in your background to be seen by others and potentially made public online. For instance, some sessions may be uploaded to websites such as YouTube. Obviously, you would need to give permission for this and would be asked to grant it. However, are you sure you want to share the things that are in the background? Many students who are on hybrid learning courses may be sharing a house or flat with fellow students. Hence what is in the background may be theirs and not yours. This is another reason why it is essential to check your background before going on to a video conference call.

Alternative backgrounds

Many video conference software programs, such as Microsoft Teams or Zoom, allow you to add "virtual backgrounds". This is where artificial intelligence determines what is in the foreground and keeps that on-screen, replacing everything else with a picture. You can either select your own image or use one supplied by the program. However, the software is not perfect. It will often think that something is in the foreground when it isn't, showing that item. Also, if you move slightly, it can think you are in the background, and so it eliminates you from the shot. Virtual backgrounds could become distracting for your fellow viewers as your image can go in and out of view if you move, even slightly. Indeed, researchers in Thailand studied online education sessions and suggested that the use of virtual backgrounds can be distracting (Ulla and Achivar, 2021). In tutorials that I have run online where people have used virtual backgrounds, there is often chat about the selected backgrounds taking time away from the topic being discussed. Plus, when people drift in and out of shot, there are interruptions as people start saying things like "Where are you?" or "You've disappeared again". Until the software is dramatically improved, virtual backgrounds are not a good idea; they cause more problems than they solve.

Green screens

If you really want to get rid of the background of your room entirely, you could use a "green screen". Although these are usually bright green, they can be any solid colour. The software for your camera can then eliminate anything that is green and replace it with an alternative image. Because the software only has to detect a single colour, replacing it is relatively easy compared with trying to replace lots of colours in your normal background. However, there are complications. Green screens need to be smooth and evenly lit. Otherwise shadows develop, and the software doesn't detect the appropriate colour, so that area is not replaced. If you don't have excellent lighting for the green screen itself, it is likely that your replacement background image will break up in places, making it distracting for your fellow students. So, even though green screens can be bought relatively cheaply, they have to be set up properly. That will take you additional time and effort, which is probably not worth it for everyday tutorial sessions. However, it could be worthwhile using a green screen when you have to record presentations for which you are being assessed. The use of a green screen can make you look more professional. Plus, you don't have to buy a professional green screen. These days I have a pop-up green screen that I can roll up behind me. However, before that, I used to have a green sheet which I pinned to the ceiling when I needed it. That cost just a few pounds and was effective. The only reason I changed to the pop-up screen was for portability so that I could make videos anywhere, rather than at my desk. If you want a green screen behind you to eliminate a background you do not want others to see, then simple things such as a green sheet may be all you need.

Background sounds

It isn't just your video background that can be distracting to your fellow students. Background noises can also be a problem. These can be reduced by getting a separate microphone that is closer to you, as explained in Chapter 2. A headset with a boom microphone can help reduce background sounds, but it will not get rid of everything. Although background images can be distracting, background sounds may be more of a problem for other students on the conference call with you. It can make students strain to hear what you are saying if the background noise distracts them (Yankelovich et al., 2006). For example, my office at home is right next door to our utility room. Before every conference call or tutorial, I have to check that the washing machine hasn't been switched on. If it has, I have to press its pause button. Otherwise, at some point in my conference call, it could go onto the spin cycle, and the noise from the room next door will distract people on the call. I remember once that I did not switch off the washing machine and one of my students wanted to know what that noise was ...!

It is, of course, possible to mute your microphone on conference calls so that any background noises do not distract others in the session. However, this leads to ever-present shouts of "You're on mute" or "Can't hear you" when a speaker forgets to unmute themselves. This can be just as distracting as the background noises. The answer is not always the mute button but a proper noise-cancelling microphone and your own attention to eliminating any background noises. That includes letting anyone else in your household know they need to be quiet when you are online in a video call. I shut my office door, and I have a sign saying "On Air" which signals to others to keep the noise down.

▶ USING VIDEO CHAT FACILITIES

All of the leading video conference programs have a chat function. This allows you to comment on the discussions taking place. As helpful as this seems, there are problems. You can't mentally focus on the words being said in the call itself and the words you read in the chat stream. You can only interpret one set of words at a time. So if you are reading what someone has said in the chat, you will not hear what is being said in the video call itself. Researchers have suggested that, when watching video, the simultaneous chat stream can be highly distracting (Weisz et al., 2007). In online tutorials, I often see students entering things into the chat, such as "Nice top you are wearing" or "I like your hair". However, when they are typing that or when others are reading it, they cannot possibly be listening to what is being said.

Use chat during video calls on a limited basis. I recommend that students only use it to ask questions if they want additional information on what is being said in the call. In other words, avoid too much "chat" and use it only for essential communication. Focus on the video call itself.

> QUICK TIP: In online video sessions, reduce your use of the chat stream to a minimum. This will allow you to focus on the call itself, and that will help your overall marks.

▶ ONLINE VIDEO ETIQUETTE

You may have witnessed bad behaviour in some of the video calls in which you have taken part. Or you may have thought that some of your fellow students are not as professional as they ought to be. Most universities will have a code of behaviour that includes online etiquette. Some universities publish separate rules about expected behaviours in online sessions. Make sure you have read those rules. Most are common sense. For example, video conference programs include a virtual "hands up" element. If you want to ask a question, you can press the "Hands Up" button, and the leader of the call will then ask you to speak. Many of the etiquette guides will ask you to do this rather than shout out or just interrupt. In face-to-face classes, students will put their hands up if they want clarification or ask a question. Or the lecturer will see they have a puzzled look on their face and will ask them if they want clarification. In online video calls, it isn't easy for the lecturer to see puzzled looks because not every student will be visible on screen in bigger classes. So some students will resort to interruption and shouting out to gain attention. The problem is that this interrupts the flow of the session for others and becomes distracting. If you have a question in online video sessions, use the "Raise Hand" button, as that will make the tutorial or seminar go more smoothly and will be less distracting to your fellow students.

Another issue of etiquette is to have your camera on during the call. You would not go into a face-to-face session with your face hidden. It is just good manners to make yourself visible to others. There is also another reason for this request in university video etiquette rules. This is so that the lecturer can see that you are actually attending. Some sessions in some universities will be compulsory. In medical schools, for instance, all classes are compulsory. If you are an international student who is engaged in hybrid learning, there may be visa requirements surrounding the level of your attendance. So, in many instances, the lecturer needs to know that you are present. However, I have known students log into a video call but not actually be present. They use one machine to log in, and then because their camera is off, they can go into another room, switch to playing a game, or even go back to bed. It would appear they are there, but they are not present. To ensure that everyone is present, etiquette rules will ask you to keep your camera switched on.

I completed a small survey of students who repeatedly switched off their cameras during video calls to find out why they were doing this. I was given several reasons such as "I haven't brushed my hair, and I look a mess" or "I'm still in bed". If you are not prepared for the video call, or you are worried about your appearance, then you need better time management to get yourself ready on time for the online session. Students would not turn up to a face-to-face session on campus without ensuring they were adequately dressed and looked presentable. So, why should it be any different for online sessions?

QUICK TIP: *Follow your university rules of online video etiquette. They are common sense and will improve your engagement.*

PRACTICAL TIPS

- **Relax.** Online video is relatively new in the world of teaching. Both lecturers and students alike are still finding their way with the technology. So, don't expect Hollywood productions and don't imagine that you need to be brilliant with video either. Everyone is still experimenting and getting used to this technology, so maybe you need to lower your expectations of what is provided for you and what you can do yourself on video.
- **Watch everything.** Even if you think you can skip recorded lectures, make sure you watch them. Evidence shows that people who watch the videos gain consistently higher marks. Plus, learning theory shows that the video enables you to understand things better.
- **Get a separate camera.** Even if your laptop comes with a good camera, you may find that an extra external camera provides you with much better images. In turn, that will improve your participation in online tutorials as the others in the group will be able to see you better.
- **Check your lighting and background.** Good lighting will improve your appearance during online video conference calls, such as tutorial sessions. The better you are seen, and the less distracting your background, the higher the level of engagement with you by others, thereby increasing your level of participation.
- **Be prepared.** When you have to join an online video conference call, make sure you are prepared. Be presentable so that you are not embarrassed when asked to keep your camera switched on.

▶ REFERENCES

Aaltonen, V., Takatalo, J., Hakkinen, J., Lehtonen, M., Nyman, G. and Schrader, M. (2009) 'Measuring Mediated Communication Experience', *2009 International Workshop on Quality of Multimedia Experience*. San Diego, CA: IEEE, pp. 104–109. DOI: 10.1109/QOMEX.2009.5246967 (Accessed: 5 October 2021).

Carmichael, M., Reid, A.-K. and Karpicke, J.D. (2018) *Assessing the Impact of Educational Video on Student Engagement, Critical Thinking and Learning: The Current State of Play*. SAGE Publishing, A Sage White Paper. Available at: https://us.sagepub.com/sites/default/files/hevideolearning.pdf (Accessed: 4 October 2021).

Costley, J. and Lange, C. (2017) 'Video Lectures in e-Learning: Effects of Viewership and Media Diversity on Learning, Satisfaction, Engagement, Interest, and Future Behavioral Intention', *Interactive Technology and Smart Education*, 14(1), pp. 14–30.

Macaranas, A., Venolia, G., Inkpen, K. and Tang, J. (2013) 'Sharing Experiences over Video: Watching Video Programs Together at a Distance', in Kotzé, P., Marsden, G., Lindgaard, G., Wesson, J. and Winckler, M. (eds) *Human–Computer Interaction – INTERACT 2013. Lecture Notes in Computer Science*. Berlin and Heidelberg: Springer-Verlag Berlin Heidelberg, pp. 73–90. DOI: 10.1007/978-3-642-40498-6_5 (Accessed: 5 October 2021).

Mayer, R.E. (2009) *Multimedia Learning*, 2nd edn. Cambridge: Cambridge University Press.

Ulla, M. and Achivar, J. (2021) 'Teaching on Facebook in a University in Thailand During the COVID-19 Pandemic: A Collaborative Autoethnographic Study', *Asia-Pacific Social Science Review*, 21(3), pp. 169–179.

Weisz, J.D., Kiesler, S., Zhang, H., Ren, Y., Kraut, R.E. and Konstan, J.A. (2007) 'Watching Together: Integrating Text Chat with Video', in *Proceedings of the SIGCHI Conference on Human Factors in Computing Systems*. San José, CA: ACM, pp. 877–886. DOI: 10.1145/1240624.1240756 (Accessed: 7 October 2021).

Yankelovich, N., Kaplan, J., Provino, J., Wessler, M. and Dimicco, J.M. (2006) 'Improving Audio Conferencing: Are Two Ears Better than One?', in *Proceedings CSCW 2006*. New York: ACM Press, pp. 333–342.

7

Effective online collaboration

Outside my office door, there is a small noticeboard. Every lecturer has a similar pinboard by the entrance to their office. We use it to post relevant information for our students, so each lecturer has different items according to the various topics they teach and their academic speciality. However, there is one thing that is standard across all these noticeboards, and it is the notification of our "office hours". These are a couple of hours each week when we guarantee we will be in our offices so that students can "drop-in" and ask questions. At other times, students would need to make an appointment as we will be lecturing, running tutorials, preparing lectures, or performing admin. The two hours posted on the noticeboards outside our offices are the guaranteed time when we are available just for students. What is interesting about these office hours is that students rarely attend alone. Usually, a small "delegation" arrives to discuss something that I said in a lecture, or to ask about their tutorial work, or perhaps to query some aspect of their assignment. This posse of students will have several questions or will all be seeking clarification of an aspect of their studies. It is rare for students to turn up to office hours on their own.

DOI: 10.4324/9781003259695-9

This is an indication that students frequently collaborate. They study together, and they ask questions together. I appreciate, of course, that sometimes the small gang that arrives in my office to ask questions are merely providing moral support for a student who is too nervous to come and seek clarification alone. They don't want to appear stupid, so they ask a group of fellow students to accompany them. However, what the fearful student might not realise is that the friends they have brought along with them also want answers to the same question but were even more scared to admit they needed help. Even if students at campus universities are not collaborating with academic questions, they join forces to provide each other with support.

For anyone studying online, this becomes much more complicated. When universities were forced to teach online during the height of the Covid pandemic, the option to join forces to support each other and ask a lecturer questions was not apparent to people. Unlike being able to turn up during office hours, the students who were forced into online study had no means of forming a little group and turning up to chat to a lecturer. Where I teach, we use Microsoft Teams as our principal online collaboration system. That has a series of symbols next to your name, which signals to other people whether you are available or not. There is a red circle to show you are busy, for example, and a green tick to indicate you are free. I told my students that my online office hours were whenever my name had a green tick against it. I suggested that all they needed to do was give me a call on Microsoft Teams whenever they saw that green tick. However, almost none of my students used this online feature. When I was on campus, my office hours were busy with students popping in for a chat, asking questions or just saying "Hi".

As soon as teaching was transferred online, that behaviour stopped. Even though I said to students that I was happy for them to call me on Microsoft Teams whenever the green tick was displayed against my name, only two students did that in the year that covered the Covid lockdowns. I had started to wonder what the problem might have been when the answer came to me when one student sent me a message asking for an appointment to speak with me. Rather than call when the green tick was displayed, this student wanted to create a Microsoft Teams calendar entry for an online meeting. Naturally, I said this was OK but added that I was perfectly happy for her to call me whenever the green tick was displayed. Her reply, though, revealed why this wasn't that attractive to students. She said that she wanted to create an online appointment so that she could invite a couple of friends to attend because they also had similar questions. It then struck me more clearly. The approach of "call me when the green tick is displayed" did not allow students to collaborate or provide moral support for one another. I thought I was providing more availability than when I was on campus. However, to the students, this was not as enticing as I might have thought. Students wanted the ability to meet me online in just the same way as they had done face-to-face, in small groups.

If you are studying entirely online and have never been on campus before, you probably will not appreciate the benefits of collaborating with other students. You will be studying alone and will only have limited opportunities to do things with your fellow learners. Yet, as my experience shows, students find that working together with others is of real help. Not only can they learn together in a shared experience, but they can also collaborate by providing moral support for each other. It is inevitable that during your studies, there will be things you do not understand or theoretical concepts you find difficult to grasp. However, like students at traditional universities, you will not want to appear stupid by asking what you might think are silly questions. That's one of the reasons why on-campus students gang together to ask those questions (which are never silly, by the way). As you saw in Chapter 1, campus-based students have many opportunities to work together and to support each other in their learning. Those chances of meeting up and working with other students are significantly reduced for distance learning. So, it is important to create ways in which you can collaborate with your colleagues, even if it is only to provide moral support for one another.

QUICK TIP: *Use every opportunity available online to connect with and collaborate with other students. It will improve your learning and make it a more enjoyable experience.*

▶ USING THE UNIVERSITY SYSTEMS FOR COLLABORATION

Your university will provide you with a range of tools for working with other students. Some of these will only be available at specific times, for instance, to allow for some assessed group work. Other features, though, will be available throughout your studies. Exactly what is provided will depend upon the systems and software selected by your particular university. Some universities, for instance, will do everything through a VLE, such as Moodle. Others will use collaboration software such as Microsoft Teams or Slack. Indeed, Slack has a system that it uses to "recreate campus life" by providing specific communication channels for socialising and collaborating. Even so, not all universities opt for such a system. Instead, they may have developed bespoke software specifically for their university requirements. Ultimately, there is no single way in which universities have chosen to create online collaboration. This means you will need to investigate the systems at your own university to ensure you know exactly what is available. When you start your studies, you will be given an induction and information about the systems you can use. However, there is a great deal of material pumped in your direction when you start university, which can be overwhelming. As a result, it is all too easy to forget what you were told about the online systems for collaboration.

QUICK TIP: *Explore all the aspects of the online systems of your university so that you can find out the various options for collaboration.*

There are several reasons why using the systems provided by the university are better than using your own methods. For a start, if you use the university's software, all of your collaborative learning is in one place. It will save you time searching through your own systems that might include a mix of social media programs, online documents, shared files, and so on. Indeed, I recall one of my students who got in a muddle just before they were due to submit a group assignment. Some of the work had been done on Google Docs, part of it had been performed using WhatsApp, and there had been discussions about the work taking place on Microsoft Teams with the chat facility there also having some of the corrections. This student wasn't sure which piece of work was the most up-to-date and was concerned he would submit the wrong one, potentially reducing his colleagues' marks. What they had ignored was the fact that I had set up a forum on Moodle (the VLE) so they could collaborate in one place, avoiding ending up in a muddle. Often, you will find that your lecturer has provided a means of collaboration. Using it will help you ensure that all your work is in one place.

There are other advantages to using university systems for collaboration when they are provided. One is that your lecturers can see you collaborating. They can monitor what is happening to make sure that everyone in the group is contributing. Many of your assessments will be based on group work. When you collaborate on that group work using the university's system, the lecturer can see if anyone has been slacking. One of the problems with group work is that students often complain that someone in the group was not pulling their weight. This is called "social loafing" and creates a sense of unfairness as the lazier student will benefit from the marks of the more active ones in the group. To counteract this, lecturers will often require collaborative group work to be conducted using the provided software provided. That way, marks can be allocated according to the amount of work contributed by each group member.

Another advantage of using the provided systems for collaboration is that lecturers can see the progress of your learning and understanding. The work you put into the system provides evidence that you are making progress. However, it also means that if you are stuck, the lecturer can see this is happening and can provide support to help you improve your understanding. If you do not use the university systems for collaboration, this kind of benefit disappears.

▶ SOCIAL MEDIA AND COLLABORATION

As you will have read in Chapter 5, social media is a valuable means of discussion and allows you to connect with other students and chat about your life at university, amongst other things. However, social media can also be used to help you work collaboratively with other students.

One of the obvious issues with being an online student is that you will not see your fellow students frequently. A significant part of campus-based interaction is where students support one another. The group work you will be asked to complete as part of your degree has two elements. First, there is the actual work itself, such as the joint assignment you need to prepare with others. Second, though, there is the mutual support and encouragement between group members that is a kind of lubricant that enables the group to work effectively and efficiently. This is where social media can step in. As already explained, you should be using university software systems for the actual collaboration. However, you could then use social media to provide your fellow group members with support and encouragement. These would be messages of praise, for instance, for work well done. There is no need to keep such messages within the collaborative system itself as they are not fundamental to the progress of the work. However, there is evidence that when students use social media to work together, there is a rise in marks of around 2 per cent (Ansari and Khan, 2020). Hence it is well worth investing some time to support each other using social media. It could well make the difference between one grade and another.

Another valuable reason for using social media is you can collaborate with experts. One of the students I taught on the MBA programme contacted me to ask if it was OK for her to get in touch with the author of one of the research papers I recommended the class read. I told the student that if she wanted to try to connect with the researcher on social media, she might find that the American professor may be willing to share further information. My student was able to get in touch with the researcher using LinkedIn. It resulted in a Zoom call where my student was able to ask several questions. It led to the student gaining a better understanding of the study in the paper as well as being able to get more up-to-date information about the progress of the research. It led to a highly impressive assignment that was given very high marks due it its unique insight. Experts are all over social media and are often willing to share their expertise. It is a form of collaboration in your studies that will enhance your learning.

> **QUICK TIP:** *Use social media to contact researchers and other experts to help you understand the subject better.*

▶ ORGANISING YOURSELF FOR ONLINE TEAMWORK

During your degree, you will be expected to collaborate with other students for a variety of group exercises, including assignments. Frequently, though, students put themselves (and the others they work with) under unnecessary pressure as they do not organise their collaborative work effectively. This leads to rushed assignments, for instance, resulting in lower grades. The notion that you can work better under pressure has been described by one psychologist as "fiction" (Knaus, 2015). Indeed, there is little evidence to support the idea that by putting things off, you will be better at them. There is plenty of support, though, for the reverse. Procrastination almost always leads to poorer results, not better ones.

There is a small group of people known as "active procrastinators". These individuals are capable of working under pressure. However, it does appear they are putting themselves under unnecessary stress. One study that looked at how students procrastinate found that those who put things off because they feel they work better under pressure only achieved the same level of results as the people who did not procrastinate (Chun Chu and Choi, 2005). In other words, believing that you work better under pressure is false. You produce the same level of results as if you were not to put off the work. All you do is make getting those results more stressful for yourself. In group work, if you put things off due to a misplaced sense of believing you work best under pressure, you are also putting your fellow students in a higher stress position. They may not be individuals who feel they work better under pressure. As a result, if you delay things, you put your colleagues under unnecessary stress. This results in poor group performance. I have lost count of the number of students who achieved lower marks than they deserved, all because their work was poor due to unnecessary delays in group work.

> QUICK TIP: If you are set group work, get on with it straight away. Delays cause stress, and there is no benefit in the misplaced belief of "working better under pressure".

Getting organised for group work, particularly as an online student, is vital. Make sure you note down all the deadlines in your diary system. Plus, sort out the dates and times for meetings with your fellow students in your group, such as Zoom calls. Put these into your calendar at the start. Even if you have nothing to talk about, meeting up online with your group members will enable you to discuss what you need to do and get to know one another better.

It is likely that any documents you need to prepare as a group will be created in a software suite such as Microsoft 365 or Google Workspace. Setting up items like folder structures, access permissions, and so on is an excellent early task in your collaboration. Otherwise, you will be part-way through the group work, and some people won't know where to find things or even be able to access them. You ought to also establish responsibilities. For instance, are you all going to proofread the document, or will that be delegated to one team member? Working out who does what at the outset will save items being missed later, thereby reducing marks if it is an assignment. For online students, all of this is much more important than for students on campus. Online you will not bump into fellow students, which campus students will do. That means if they have forgotten something for their group work, they can remind a colleague as they pass in the corridor between lectures. As an online student, you will not have that opportunity, so being organised from the outset for collaborative work is essential.

▶ PROJECT MANAGEMENT TOOLS

There is a wide variety of project management software and apps you can use online to help with collaborative work. These can be used to help ensure everyone is on track and that each element of the work has been done on time. However, for many straightforward group assignments, such systems can be more trouble than they are worth. You can spend hours administering the system instead of just getting on with your work.

There are, though, some online tools that are straightforward and will help you see at a glance the progress of your group work. One particular style of an app which can achieve this uses what is known as the Kanban style. Kanban is a visual scheduling billboard that was developed in Japan for the car manufacturer Toyota (Ohno, 1988). This is a rapid method of being able to see at what stage each element of the process is and what remaining work needs to be done.

You start a Kanban board with all the items in the first column, the To Do list. You can then have as many columns to the right as

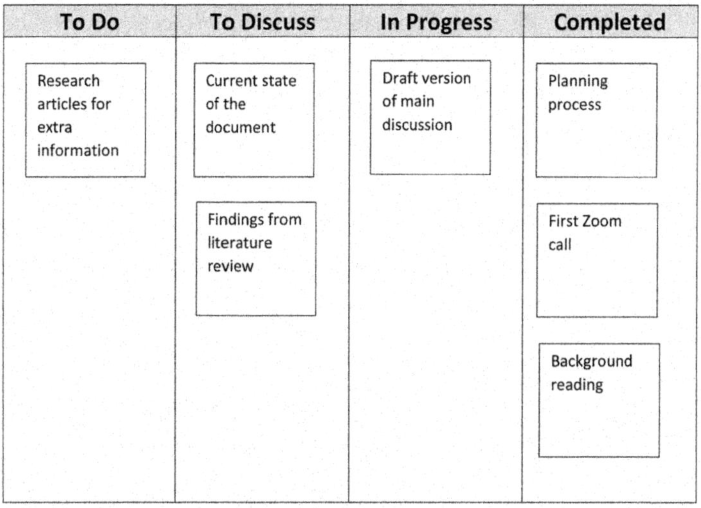

To Do	To Discuss	In Progress	Completed
Research articles for extra information	Current state of the document	Draft version of main discussion	Planning process
	Findings from literature review		First Zoom call
			Background reading

Figure 7.1 A Kanban-style progress checker

necessary, depending upon the various stages you might have. The last column is the Completed column, which is where you place things that have been done. Many people use physical Kanban boards and move sticky notes across from one column to the next as work progresses. However, as an online student, you need to be able to see the board together with your fellow group members. Hence, you need an online Kanban board.

Trello

Trello is one of the most popular online Kanban board systems. It is available in a variety of versions. The free one is perfectly adequate for running student collaborations. There are other more popular systems, but they are focused on business teams, and some are relatively costly. Trello, however, can be free of charge and is more suited to small groups than the higher-ranked competition. Trello also has smartphone apps, making it particularly useful for students. Indeed, the Trello blog has several articles explaining how students can get the best out of this planning software

(Trello, 2021). By using Trello in your group projects, you will be able to manage all of the tasks more efficiently, helping to ensure you get your work done on time and to a good standard.

Alternatives to Trello

There are many alternatives to Trello. Some require payment. Some are complicated and require some setting up and learning. You can find a list of alternatives on the website I have created to accompany this book, https://studyingonline.tips. Two of the most widely used alternatives, which offer more than just Kanban planning, are Airtable and ClickUp. These competing systems provide a highly sophisticated method of project management, but both are available in free versions, so they may be worthwhile exploring.

▶ WHEN YOU SHOULD NOT COLLABORATE

It is all too easy for students to collaborate. This is especially the case for online students with ready access to systems such as Microsoft Teams or social media apps. This presents a potential problem. Your degree needs to be assessed on your work. After all, it is you that will get those all-important letters after your name. Yet, if you have collaborated to obtain those qualifications, you will have cheated. You will have cheated your future employers, for instance. They will believe you have a level of skills, knowledge, and understanding that may not be true. If you have collaborated with other students, some of the work for which you receive marks will have been completed by them, not you. You will also be cheating yourself. After all, you will believe you are better than is the case because your higher marks will have come about as a result of working with others.

Collaborating with others for individual work is a serious academic offence. Indeed, your university will have an Academic Integrity

Code or a Code of Student Conduct that will indicate penalties for collaborating on individual work. This can include expulsion from the university without a qualification. Universities have several methods in place for detecting collaboration. There is even artificial intelligence (AI) that can detect differences in writing styles. This would mean that if part of your work had been written by someone else, these AI systems would spot the difference between your words and those from a collaborator. Not only are you cheating yourself when you collaborate on individual work, but you also run the risk of severe penalties that could affect your entire future.

> **QUICK TIP:** Only collaborate with other students on group exercises and group work set by your lecturers.

However, lecturers will want you to collaborate for tutorial discussions, for instance, or for other group exercises. As explained at the start of this chapter, there is plenty of evidence that shows when you collaborate with other students, your understanding and ability to evaluate things critically goes up. In other words, collaboration is good for your academic thinking. That means it is good to discuss things with fellow students. It is helpful to work with them on improving knowledge and understanding. It is just not a good idea to extend that collaboration so you work jointly on elements of your assessment that are individual. You want to be assessed for what you know, not for what others know.

PRACTICAL TIPS

- **Check out university systems for collaboration.** Your university is likely to have a variety of software programs that can be used for collaboration with other students on group work. Make sure you get to know these systems. There are several advantages to using these systems rather than your own.
- **Use social media for collaboration.** Social media can enhance your group work by encouraging and supporting fellow students.

- **Start collaboration early.** The sooner you start group work, the better. Don't delay; this just adds to stress and can lead to lower marks.
- **Use an online project management tool.** Get software that allows you to share the progress of work being done by each team member. Kanban-style software is available on the web and in apps that provide an easy way to keep group work on track.
- **Only collaborate when asked.** Avoid collaborating to help you with your individual work. You will be assessed for work you have not done, which can lead to severe penalties and consequences.

▶ REFERENCES

Ansari, J.A.N. and Khan, N.A. (2020) 'Exploring the Role of Social Media in Collaborative Learning the New Domain of Learning', *Smart Learning Environments*, 7(1), p. 9.

Chun Chu, A.H. and Choi, J.N. (2005) 'Rethinking Procrastination: Positive Effects of "Active" Procrastination Behavior on Attitudes and Performance', *The Journal of Social Psychology*, 145(3), pp. 245–264.

Knaus, W. (2015) 'The Procrastination Fallacy of Working Better Under Pressure', *Psychology Today*. Available at: www.psychologytoday.com/gb/blog/science-and-sensibility/201508/the-procrastination-fallacy-working-better-under-pressure (Accessed: 17 October 2021).

Ohno, T. (1988) *Toyota Production System: Beyond Large-Scale Production*. Boca Raton, FL: Productivity Press.

Trello (2021) 'Trello Blog | Helping Teams Work Better, Together'. Available at: https://blog.trello.com (Accessed: 17 October 2021).

8

Coping with online presentations

Students are required to give all kinds of presentations during their studies. These vary from simply talking in a tutorial to provide an insight into a specific question right through to formal presentations that are assessed as part of their degree. You will be expected to present your ideas to class regularly. Inevitably, students are wary and often scared of making presentations. They are not alone. In one study of what people are frightened about, public speaking was top of the list. Being scared of dying was third on the list. So, people appear to be more scared of giving a presentation than meeting their demise. This was explored in a book written by two friends of mine called *And Death Came Third* (Roper and Lopata, 2011). It highlighted the need to get to grips with speaking in public and eradicating the fear of doing so. Whatever career you choose after university, giving presentations is going to play an important part. Indeed, the higher up the career ladder you go, the more critical presentations become. This is one of the reasons why universities incorporate presenting within their modules. It is a means of preparing you for the world of work.

However, students frequently find presenting in class scary. During my time as a lecturer, I have had to encourage, coax, and

DOI: 10.4324/9781003259695-10

counsel students who have been in various states of fear about presenting. Occasionally, I've had to refer students to the university's well-being team so that they can gain professional counselling or therapy for their extreme state of fear. Fortunately, that is rare. However, if you are horribly frightened by making presentations, support is available.

> **QUICK TIP:** *If you have an extreme fear of making presentations, contact your university's counselling service. They will provide you with coping strategies.*

For students on the campus, they will be expected to make presentations face-to-face in a classroom or lecture theatre. That can be particularly frightening because students are out of their comfort zone. Usually, they would be sitting in class with all eyes on the lecturer. Now, they are in the front of the class, with all their fellow students looking at them. Plus, if the presentation is assessed, the student knows that their lecturer is taking notes and finding things that could be wrong with what they are doing. For students who are studying at home, via the Internet, it might seem that it is less frightening. That is not the case. You might be in a more comfortable environment, such as sitting at the desk in your bedroom. However, what you see on the screen are all the faces of the rest of the class staring right at you. In fact, being scared of online presenting is so common these days it has a special name. It is called "Zoom anxiety". In one study of this phenomenon, 73 per cent of people who were involved in online meetings suffered from this issue (Buffalo 7, 2020). It simply isn't the case that because you are in familiar surroundings, sitting at home, that you won't be anxious about making presentations. People who have to present online have just the same kind of fears as those students who make presentations in a physical classroom.

▶ OVERCOMING PRESENTATION FEARS

Most students will get anxious about any kind of presentation. Reducing or removing that anxiety can make your studies more enjoyable, plus it will help you gain higher marks if the presentation is being assessed. To understand how to deal with the fear of presenting, it's essential to realise how it arises. It is a fundamental biological instinct. People who tell you they never get nervous at presenting are either fibbing or think that their biological response to making presentations is normal, so it doesn't phase them.

Deep inside your brain is a system that is designed to ensure you survive. It deals with all kinds of biological feedback from your body to ensure that all your systems are working correctly. If it detects something is wrong, it can do things to put it right. For instance, you go out for a walk and twist your ankle. The body detects something is wrong, a pain signal is triggered, and, in return, that stops you from using your ankle. It's a system that protects against further damage while your body repairs the problem. Within this system there are also responses to deal with situations that are unknown or unpredictable. Your brain knows the standard everyday stuff you encounter and can see it is no danger to your survival. But if you enter some unusual space that you have never been to before, your brain doesn't know if this is a threat to your survival until it has done some other checks. For example, imagine you have walked into a building that is very, very hot. Your body will detect the temperature change and will trigger perspiration. Your survival instinct in your brain notices this and starts to check if other problems could exist. Your sight and hearing might be made more acute, for instance. After all, there is the possibility that the building is on fire or that the heating system is about to explode. Because your brain is not sure what is going on, it prepares your body to do one of two things until it gets more information. Either you need to run out of there as fast as you can, or you need to deal with the issue causing the heat in the room. This means you need to either take on the problem or run away. It is known as the "fight or flight" response.

If you are going to run away or deal with a significant issue, your body needs one thing above all others – muscle power. Because your brain does not know how much muscle power you will need or when you are going to require it, the survival instinct prepares you for almost instantaneous activity. That means once the systems have detected what you need to do in this unusual situation, your muscles can immediately go into overdrive. To help achieve this, your bodily defence mechanisms trigger a significant release of a hormone called adrenalin (also known as epinephrine). This changes where your blood is circulating. During a typical day, much of your blood is in your gut, helping to process food and in your head to help your brain. However, your body may need lots of energy in the muscles, so adrenaline opens up the blood vessels in your muscles and closes them down in the core of your body. At the same time, because you will need more oxygen, adrenaline triggers an increase in your respiration rate. It also raises your heart rate so that more blood is pumped around the body.

The problem for your survival instincts is that they do not know the difference between the threat of being in a potentially burning building and the danger of sitting in front of a screen full of people all staring at you waiting for you to speak. When you are about to give a presentation, whether it is face-to-face or online, your "fight or flight" response will kick in, and your adrenaline levels will rise. If you were in a burning building, you would run away. Your body would then know the danger had passed, and the adrenaline production would stop because you are back in safety. The muscular activity is a signal to the brain that the adrenaline has worked.

Think about that for a moment. If muscular activity is a sign that adrenaline is no longer needed, this suggest that in the case of presenters sitting still at their desk their adrenaline will continue to be pumped out. I am sure you will have seen some presenters who are "rabbits in the headlights". They are rooted to the spot, staring forward, seemingly unable to do anything. That's because their adrenaline is pumping away, and their brain is telling them this is increasingly scary, partly because it hasn't detected any muscular activity. As soon as you move, adrenaline levels fall.

If you are making presentations in class, this means it is easy to feel less scared. All you need to do is to move about. When

I am lecturing students face-to-face, I move about a lot. I wander around the platform, and I even get off the stage and walk around the lecture room. Students feel more engaged because I get closer to them. However, I am also feeling better because my brain senses the muscular movement and cuts adrenaline production, which would otherwise make me anxious.

Overcoming fear of presenting online

What can you do, though, if you are presenting online? You are sitting still at your desk, unable to move. If your brain thinks this is a fight or flight situation and there is no muscular activity, you will just get more and more scared. The answer to this is to use biology to your advantage. What you need to do is to get your adrenaline levels lowered before you start. If your body starts at a lower adrenaline level when you begin your online presentation, you won't have as much anxiety. Even if you remain static in your chair and your adrenaline levels rise, they won't go too high. But how do you lower your base adrenaline levels? The answer is exercise. It provides lots of muscular activity, lowering your adrenaline production. So, if you are due to make an online presentation get some exercise immediately before your time slot. The best way of doing this is to go for a brisk 20-minute walk half an hour before your presentation time. You should walk fast enough to make your heart pound a bit and to produce some sweat. You will then have ten minutes to recover before your presentation. However, your adrenaline levels will be lower, and so you will be less anxious. In addition, the walk will have led to a rise of another kind of hormone in your body known as "endorphins". These help make you feel more relaxed. Hence, some vigorous exercise in the half-hour before a presentation will make you feel much less nervous.

QUICK TIP: Whenever you have to present online, ensure you get 20 minutes of brisk exercise in the half-hour before. It will reduce your nervousness significantly.

It might seem unlikely that something as simple as going for a walk will reduce your nervousness. In several tests of this, both with students and people in business, I have found it produces a real impact. For instance, in one class, I asked everyone to rate their nervousness at the start of the session in which they were due to make a presentation. Then I asked one group to give their presentations immediately and rate their nervousness after they had finished speaking. However, with the second group of students, I sent them out for a walk. I then asked them to rate their nervousness when they got back into the room and once again after they had finished speaking.

The students in both groups reported a similar fall in nervousness once it was all over. However, the group who had exercised started with a lower level of nervousness. Overall, not only were those who exercised less nervous, the fall in anxiety after a presentation meant that the experience was more enjoyable. It is clear that exercise has a real impact on your presentation anxiety. Indeed, other researchers have discovered the impact of exercise on reducing anxiety (Wood et al., 2018).

Moving while presenting online

You can get the benefits of muscular movement while you are presenting online, even if you are sitting in your chair at your desk. Move your feet back and forth, swinging your legs under the desk.

TABLE 8.1 Impact of exercise on ratings of nervousness before and after presenting

	Nervousness before presentation	Nervousness after presentation
No exercise before presentation	9	7
20 minutes' exercise before presentation	6	4

You can also use your arms to gesture. Often, people get stuck staring at the camera, not moving their arms. However, moving your arms and gesturing, combined with the movement of your legs, will help keep that adrenaline level low, thereby reducing your sense of nervousness. People tend to think they need to keep still when facing a camera and so they do not move. However, take a look at those relaxed TV presenters you see, such as newsreaders. They do not sit perfectly still; they move their body. It seems natural to us. However, when we go in front of a camera in an online presentation, we tend to think we need to keep perfectly still. In a study of what students preferred in terms of online presentations, one point made was about a desire for presenters to move (Olsen, 2021). Indeed, when I ask students whether they prefer people on screen who move and gesture or people who sit perfectly still, they always plump for the individual who moves about. So, don't fall into the trap of sitting still when you present online. Move as it will make the people watching more engaged with what you are saying. Plus, your nervousness and anxiety will go down due to reduced adrenalin levels.

▶ OTHER WAYS OF REDUCING PRESENTATION ANXIETY

There is a wide variety of advice on getting rid of presentation nervousness. This ranges from "imagine your audience is naked" to hypnosis. The imagine people naked idea is, frankly, bonkers. It has no impact on your state of anxiety. Indeed, it can make things worse as you become embarrassed at about the thought of people in the room with no clothes on. The last thing a student wants to consider is their elderly professor naked. Hypnotherapy certainly works for people with extreme fear of public speaking, a condition called "glossophobia". However, regular hypnotherapy sessions cost money, so with limited student funds available, it is probably better not to consider hypnosis unless your presentation anxiety is extreme.

The anxiety you suffer is a primary biological response, so it is better to choose biological methods to deal with nervousness.

Exercise, of course, is an ideal way. However, people who practise yoga have also been shown to have lower anxiety levels when speaking in public (Radecki, 2020). Yoga is known to trigger a range of biological responses within the body. It is a natural way to help reduce anxiety levels.

> **QUICK TIP:** *Take up yoga classes if you suffer from bouts of anxiety when presenting. Regular yoga has been shown to cut public speaking nervousness.*

Other biological impacts on anxiety can be produced by practising mindfulness. Mindfulness itself is explored further in Chapter 11. However, for public speaking, mindfulness techniques have been shown to help in a range of different anxiety-provoking situations (Hoge et al., 2013). Furthermore, in research on students from Thailand who were asked to make presentations in English, mindfulness was a clear help in reducing anxiety (Charoensukmongkol, 2019). Researchers have found that mindfulness has a direct biological effect on the brain (Powell, 2018). One of the fundamental methods of mindfulness that works well for presentation nervousness is a simple breathing exercise. Sit still in a quiet room and close your eyes. Breathe in and out slowly. Concentrate on listening to the breath going in through your nose and out through your mouth. Focus on that noise and try to stop your mind from wandering. It will, but just keep bringing your attention back to the breath itself. As you breathe in, count to four before exhaling for a count of eight. The time it takes for you to breathe out is twice as long as your breath in, you will feel calmer.

Some additional methods of making sure you reduce your presentation nerves will also help. They are not biological, but will make you feel better. The top of the list is preparation. If you are not prepared, you will inevitably feel nervous. Make sure you know what is expected of you for the presentation. Check the assignment instructions carefully if the presentation is assessed. One excellent student I taught lost significant marks on their presentation because they missed a necessary instruction. Even though their presentation was very good, they realised they had missed out a critical component, and so that increased their nerves and led to a loss of marks.

An essential component of preparation is practice. When I ask students how many times they have practised their presentation, they usually tell me "once or twice". However, I used to be the Chief Executive Officer of the Professional Speaking Association (PSA) in the UK. The members of that organisation earn their living by being paid to speak in public at conferences and business events. When I asked the top earners in the PSA how many times they practise their speeches, they told me "hundreds". I also used to work backstage in a theatre, so I met several actors. I asked them how many times they rehearsed each scene. They told me "thousands". You can see where this is heading. The professionals who appear in public practise many more times than students who are asked to present in public.

> **QUICK TIP:** *Practise your presentation more times than you think is necessary. The more practice you can fit in, the less nervous you will be.*

One other important method of reducing your presentation nerves is to get honest feedback from someone you trust. Once you are reasonably confident you are adequately prepared and have already done some practice, get a friend to watch you. They will tell you what is good about what you are doing and give you some tips on delivery. This will help reduce your nerves when it comes to the real thing because you already know you are doing well and that you have improved upon what you were planning due to the feedback. Several years ago, I had to give an important speech in front of a couple of hundred people. I was nervous, despite being an experienced lecturer and public speaker used to standing in front of audiences of all sizes. Even so, I asked two of my friends to listen to me rehearse my speech. They suggested

I change just one thing. But that small change made all the difference. Not only did it provide more impact for the speech, but it also made me less nervous about what I was saying. If you are due to make an online presentation, it is even easier for you to get someone to watch one of your rehearsals. They can join you on a video phone call. Or you could record your practice session and send them the video to watch.

▶ THE DIFFICULTIES OF PRESENTING ONLINE

One of the critical differences between face-to-face presenting and presenting online is that you are less able to move around. Indeed, most of the time, you will be sitting down. That's not typical for a presenter. Usually, presentations are made while you are standing up. Depending on the technology you are using, you may be forced to sit down. In Chapter 2, you will have read that buying a separate webcam is a good idea. If you do that, you can add it to a small desktop tripod. That means you can stand up when presenting online, which will make you feel more natural. It will also give you more energy and improve your voice due to it being easier to breathe when standing. If you continue to use the webcam attached to your monitor or laptop, you will be forced to sit down to present.

> *QUICK TIP: Use a stand-alone webcam so that you can mount it on a tripod, which will allow you to stand up when presenting.*

Another issue with online presenting is that you have to manage technology while trying to talk. Generally, in face-to-face presentations, your only technology would be a handheld clicker to move through the slides. For online presenting, though, you have to ensure you can be seen and heard. You need to arrange screen sharing, click through the slides, and keep an eye on the chat. That's before you even think about uploading the slides for others to download so they can annotate them for their notes. You might even be asked to use online "polling" software for interactivity with the rest of the class. The result of all this is that you are required to be something of a technical wizard all the time you are trying to make a presentation.

> QUICK TIP: *Explore all the features of your online presentation software and practise using it. That way, you will be able to concentrate on giving your talk, rather than getting distracted by finding out how to achieve something with the program.*

For many students, there will be group work to complete and present. This group work can be part of a tutorial session, for example. Or it could be a team assignment in which everyone in the group is assessed together. When you are all in the same room, giving a group presentation is relatively easy. You can all see each other, and one of you can step in if they notice one of their colleagues is struggling. Equally, being in the same room means you can more easily support one another and provide encouragement. When you are all in separate places because you are studying online, a group presentation becomes more difficult. You need to have practised more when you have to do a group presentation online. Not only will you need to think about timings more carefully, but also who will operate the slides if you have them or who will run the screen share. If you haven't sorted this out in advance, your online presentation will not go smoothly.

> QUICK TIP: *For group, presentations make sure that you have planned the technical nature of your talk and practised in advance. Otherwise, it will look disjointed and not seem like a single presentation.*

There is one other significant difference between presenting online and face-to-face. When you are in a room with other people, you pick up on their energy. If you are doing well with your presentation, you will feel it and sense it from the atmosphere in the room. People will be leaning forward, smiling, and showing they are interested. As the presenter, you notice this, and it fills you with energy. It improves your confidence as well. Earlier I mentioned that I used to work in the theatre and would often speak with actors. They all seemed to agree that no matter how many rehearsals they had undertaken, performing in front of an audience made them better. Somehow, people being in the same room enhances what they do. University lecturers say the same. When there are students in the room, the lecture is always better than the rehearsal. We somehow pick up on the energy, and it improves performance. So, presenting online is problematic. There is no one in the room to receive some kind of energy from. Even if you can see people on the screen, they are not necessarily looking at you. Besides, many will have their cameras off while they are listening. Plus, sometimes the software will only show you a selection of the people watching, rather than everyone. This makes presenting online more challenging than giving a presentation face-to-face. As an online student, you are going to have to make several presentations via the web. So you will need to find a way of gaining energy from the room when everyone in that room is separate. The best way of doing this is to make your presentation interactive. Ask questions so that people have to answer. Get them to add things to the chat. Use polls within the video call program so that people can vote on things. Look for ways you can make your presentation interactive, and you will get a greater sense of involvement by the people online. That, in turn, will boost your energy in much the same way that energy is boosted when everyone is in the same room together.

> QUICK TIP: *Make your online presentations as interactive as possible. That will help everyone feel more involved, but it also boosts you as you get to sense their involvement.*

Do not get too concerned, though, about online presenting. In my experience, students appear to prefer it to standing up in front of a class. Indeed, last year when I gave students a choice of presenting online or face-to-face, the majority opted for using web-based video presentations. A study completed in the USA a few years ago also found a preference for online presentations (Thor et al., 2017).

▶ PLANNING AND PREPARING ONLINE PRESENTATIONS

Earlier in this chapter, you will have read about the need to prepare presentations properly if you are to avoid a sense of nervousness. There is much more to consider when planning an online presentation than when you are doing a similar talk face-to-face. When the Coronavirus pandemic hit the UK, like many lecturers, I was forced to teach online. It took me much longer to prepare my online lectures than it ever did for an on-campus one. I mentioned this to a friend of mine whose daughter had been complaining to him about the lack of value she was getting for her student fees at university. She was upset that all she got was recorded lectures, and there was no chance to interact with the lecturers and professors. I explained that typically it would take twice as long to prepare a lecture as the time slot provided. So a two-hour lecture would require four hours of preparation time. However, as I told my friend, to prepare two hours of lecture material online takes about 12 hours. In other words, it takes three times longer to prepare online lectures than face-to-face ones. What was taking around half a day for face-to-face was taking almost two days for the online version. My friend said he was going straight back to his daughter to explain and to help her realise why she ought not to complain ... !

I tell you this not to make you feel any sympathy for lecturers and their demanding job. Rather, it is to help you realise that you also need more time to prepare online presentations. In an on-campus face-to-face presentation, for instance, the interactivity often happens spontaneously. People ask questions, or you notice something and interact with the others in the room. That doesn't happen online anything like as frequently as it takes place face-to-face. As a result, you need to build interactivity into your presentation, for example, by creating a poll or a chat-based exercise. Those elements of interactivity need preparation as they do not happen spontaneously. Hence you need more time to prepare your online presentations.

Another part of the planning and preparation that is required for online presentations, but not face-to-face ones, is knowing what you can and cannot do with the software. Also, you may need to find add-ons and extensions to achieve particular elements. For example, if you are using Microsoft Teams and want to run a poll, it is not built directly into the program. You need to use one of the available add-ons to include a poll. That means you need to select one of the available options, install it, and test it for suitability. This all adds time to preparing your work.

> **QUICK TIP: Make sure you understand the features available in your video call software so that you can make the best possible presentation.**

There is another issue with online presentations that does not affect face-to-face presentations to the same extent. In a face-to-face presentation, people can more easily look away from your slides. They can look at you, for example. They can also look at each other. In other words, they do not have to constantly stare at your slides. This means that if you keep the same slide visible for a few minutes, it does not matter too much. However, online when a slide is shown for too long, it becomes tedious and distracting. People probably cannot look at you when you are screen sharing. It does depend on the software being used, but mostly your image is reduced to a much smaller size so that people can focus on the presentation slides themselves. If you are chatting away and the slides have been on screen for several minutes, people will disconnect from what you are saying. For an online presentation, you need many more slides than for the same presentation face-to-face. You need to be changing the visuals frequently. Consider a drama TV programme you like or a soap opera you watch. The image changes regularly. First, you see a couple of people in a scene together. Then there is a close up of one of them. After that, you are looking over the shoulder of the other person. Then there's a wide-angle shot of the whole scene. This constant changing of view is what helps keep us hooked and watching. If the shot is shown for too long, the TV companies know that people drift away. Indeed, they have research that shows how much attention people are paying at any single moment. This has helped them understand the importance of regular changes in perspective to keep the audience watching. For online presentations, you are in a similar situation. If you do not keep changing the visuals, your audience will also drift away. You know yourself that when you have been watching an online presentation, it has happened to you. Don't go pretending you have never checked your emails while you were supposed to be watching an online presentation. That kind of behaviour happens when the online presentation remains static. You want to avoid this happening when you are presenting. So, in your preparation, make sure you have plenty of visuals that change regularly to keep your audience hooked.

> **QUICK TIP:** *You need many more slides and visuals for an online presentation than you might include in a face-to-face talk.*

There is one other aspect of online presentations that also needs consideration: the issue of "cognitive overload". This happens when you provide too much information or ask your audience to do too many things at once. When planning to present over the web, you need to consider this. If you are going to have a slide with several bullet points on it and you are asking your audience to take part in a poll while looking at the slide, there's a danger that is too much for them to hold in their mind at the same time. This leads to cognitive overload, and they will either not read the slide or not participate in the poll. So, you need to consider carefully how you will present your information online. Not only is doing things like showing text slides and polls simultaneously something of an issue but there are other potential areas for cognitive overload. For example, if you are asking people to use the chat, you need to stop talking. They cannot type and listen at the same time. Similarly, if you are asking the audience to look at some data on a document you have uploaded, you cannot expect them to do that at the same time as looking at some slides. You need to prepare your online presentations so that your audience is effectively only doing one thing at a time. Otherwise, they will suffer from cognitive overload, and your presentation will not have the impact you wanted.

▶ DEALING WITH RECORDED PRESENTATIONS

Not all of your presentations will be live. You will often be required to record a presentation and upload it to the VLE. This is particularly the case if your presentation is going to be assessed. Recordings mean that assessment can be fairer as two or more lecturers can assess the presentation and agree on a mark. Also, it means that external examiners can verify the assessment of presentations to make sure everything is fair. With face-to-face presentations, that isn't possible. So, you can expect to be asked to record presentations. Quite how you will be asked to do this can vary, depending upon the lecturer's requirements. For example, in a group presentation, you may be asked to record a Zoom call or a Microsoft Teams meeting. Or you may simply be asked to record a PowerPoint presentation. Sometimes, it will not even be a video recording. You may be asked to record audio only, like a podcast. Indeed, I include a podcast recording as one of the assessments in a module I teach. The students are put into groups of three, and they are expected to record an audio discussion of a specific topic, rather like a chat show style radio programme.

Organising your recording is relatively straightforward as long as you have thoroughly checked the requirements. Students often get into difficulty with recordings because they haven't read the instructions properly. This wastes time and can also lead to a reduction in marks if you produce the material incorrectly. Like so many other aspects of assessment, checking the instructions is fundamental. For recorded presentations, it is particularly important. The last thing you want to do is to be forced to re-record something because you did it incorrectly the first time.

Recording PowerPoint

Making a recording of a PowerPoint presentation is possible using the system built in to the program. Once you have completed your PowerPoint slides and you know what you want to say, you can go to the "Recording" menu and press the "Record Slide Show" button. If the "Recording" menu is not visible, click on "Options", select "Customise Ribbon", and then in the right-hand column, you can select "Recording" to make it visible.

Once you have pressed the recording button, the screen will change, and you will see the "Slide Show" version of your slides. There are icons that allow you to switch the audio and camera on and off, though I have no idea why you would want to do that if you are making a video recording. Once you are happy with the settings, you can press the record icon, you will get a countdown on the screen, and you can then begin speaking and click through the slides. The system also allows you to use highlighting and a laser pointer while you are talking so that you can point out specific elements of your slides. Once you have finished, you can save the presentation, and you will see your video image in the bottom right of each slide. When the presentation is run in Slide Show form, your video and sound are automatically played, and the slides are moved forward.

QUICK TIP: Save your PowerPoint recorded presentations using the "Save As" option and save them as a MPEG-4 video file. That way, the video presentation can be viewed more easily. You can even upload it to YouTube.

Recording Google Slides

Unlike PowerPoint, Google Slides does not have an in-built recording system. Instead, you either need to get an add-on for Google Slides or use another recording method. A common way of doing this is with screen recording software. There are plenty of programs around that do this. You can find a list on the website I have created to accompany this book, https://studyingonline. tips. Also, there are specific "lecture capture" systems that work with Google Slides to enable you to record your presentation. Two of the most popular programs are Panopto (www.panopto.com) and Loom (www.loom.com). Both of these have options allowing you to record several hours of video free of charge. All you do is load your Google Slides presentation, switch to the recording software, and then share the presentation. Your presentation is then recorded alongside your webcam and microphone. If you don't want to get extra software, you could also export your Google Slides presentation into PowerPoint format and record the presentation using that program's recording option.

Saving recorded presentations

One issue with many recorded presentations is that there is a period at the start when people are checking everything is working. You can sometimes hear people asking if it is all working or muttering to themselves as they set things up. At the end of the video, there is frequently a period of time where you can see the presenter looking around, clearly clicking through things on the screen before finally hitting the "Stop" button. It all looks rather unprofessional. To avoid this, you need to edit the video's start and end to ensure it looks the best you can make it. Remember, you are being assessed on these recorded presentations, so it is important to make them as good as possible.

In PowerPoint, you can select the first slide, click on the video image in the corner, and then select "Trim Video" from the "Playback" menu. Just play the video and check where it really begins. You can then move the "Start" slider to that position, trimming off the nonsense at the start. You can do a similar thing for the last slide, but this time trimming off the material after the presentation itself has finished. Doing this will tidy up the start and end of your presentation video, improving how it is perceived.

Of course, you can go to all kinds of lengths to edit the video and add a range of features to it, such as captions and fancy graphics. Unless you are on a media course, where you will inevitably have access to proper video editing software, it is highly unlikely that doing anything sophisticated with your presentation video will have any impact on your marks. However, if you want to stand out or take some pride in your work, there are free online video editing programs that can help you spruce up your work. Two that are often used by students are Clipchamp (https://clipchamp.com/en) and WeVideo (www.wevideo.com).

Consider presentation file sizes

When recording videos, one issue you will need to take care of is the file size. Recorded presentations can be very large indeed. Many VLEs will have size limits for the files you need to upload for assessments. This could mean that your recorded presentation is too large to submit. There are a few ways around this problem.

One way of reducing file size is to convert the item to a different format. There are plenty of video and file conversion programs that you can download free of charge. You may need to experiment a bit, but often by saving to a different acceptable format, you can reduce the file size significantly.

Another way of dealing with the file size is to create a "Zip" file. This is a compressed form of the file that can save space. On a Windows PC, you just right click on the file and choose "Send To" and select "Compressed (Zipped) file". On a Mac, you control-click on the file and choose "Compress". You can then upload the smaller zipped file to your VLE.

Sometimes, though, even if you have edited the video to its smallest time frame, swapped the format to one that is smaller, and zipped the file, it is still too big to upload. Depending on what your lecturer wants, there are a few alternatives. You could use a large file sharing service or put the item in your cloud, such as Google Drive or Microsoft OneDrive. Another option is to upload the presentation video to your YouTube account but use the settings to make the video "Unlisted". That way, only people with the link will be able to view it. Your video is still public, but it isn't displayed in the usual way. You can then send the "secret" link to your lecturer instead of the video file. I often ask students to do this as it saves them time having to concern themselves with file sizes.

> **QUICK TIP:** *Keep your file sizes small by setting your webcam to 780p rather than 1080p. This will help reduce the size of your video footage.*

PRACTICAL TIPS

- **Allow plenty of time for preparation**. Online presenting is more complex than making face-to-face presentations. You will need to consider a range of technical matters and help your online viewers avoid cognitive overload. All of this requires more planning and more practical work on your part. You will need about three times the amount of time it would take you to prepare the same presentation for a face-to-face situation.
- **Take steps to avoid nervousness**. Exercise, yoga, and mindfulness will help reduce your nerves. The way online presentations work, with you being static, means it is easier to get more nervous than for on-campus presenting. Hence, it is vital to do all you can to avoid the inevitable anxiety of presenting.

- **Get a separate webcam on a tripod.** Presenting from a chair is not as easy as presenting standing up. However, webcams attached to screens make it almost impossible to stand. If you have a separate webcam on a desktop tripod, you can stand when presenting. That will make you more comfortable and improve your voice as you breathe better when standing.
- **Make your online presentations interactive.** An interactive presentation is more engaging for the audience. However, it is crucial for you as an online presenter. With interaction, you get a sense of viewer participation. This boosts your energy as you realise people are engaging with your material.
- **Make your recordings professional.** Use software to trim the start and end of your video to improve its professionalism. PowerPoint can do this for you. Or there are free online video editing programs that can help.

▶ REFERENCES

Buffalo 7 (2020) 'Biggest Triggers of Zoom Anxiety | Video Call Fatigue', Buffalo 7. Available at: https://buffalo7.co.uk/blog/zoom-anxiety (Accessed: 30 October 2021).

Charoensukmongkol, P. (2019) 'The Role of Mindfulness in Reducing English Language Anxiety among Thai College Students', *International Journal of Bilingual Education and Bilingualism*, 22(4), pp. 414–427.

Hoge, E.A., Bui, E., Marques, L., Metcalf, C.A., Morris, L.K., Robinaugh, D.J., Worthington, J.J., Pollack, M.H. and Simon, N.M. (2013) 'Randomized Controlled Trial of Mindfulness Meditation for Generalised Anxiety Disorder: Effects on Anxiety and Stress Reactivity', *The Journal of Clinical Psychiatry*, 74(8), pp. 786–792.

Olsen, D. (2021) 'The Impact of Camera Angles in Learning Videos on the Perception of Teaching Excellence and Emotional Connectedness of Students in the Creative Industries', *Compass: Journal of Learning and Teaching*, 14(1), pp. 110–120.

Powell, A. (2018) 'Harvard Researchers Study How Mindfulness May Change the Brain in Depressed Patients', *Harvard Gazette*. Available at: https://news.harvard.edu/gazette/story/2018/04/harvard-researchers-study-how-mindfulness-may-change-the-brain-in-depressed-patients (Accessed: 30 October 2021).

Radecki, S. (2020) 'Yoga and Public Speaking Anxiety: Bringing the Mind–Body Connection to the Center', *Communication Center Journal*, 6(1), pp. 112–115.

Roper, P. and Lopata, A. (2011) *And Death Came Third*, 2nd edn. St Albans: Ecademy Press.

Thor, D., Xiao, N., Zheng, M., Ma, R. and Yu, X.X. (2017) 'An Interactive Online Approach to Small-Group Student Presentations and Discussions', *Advances in Physiology Education*, 41(4), pp. 498–504.

Wood, C.J., Clow, A., Hucklebridge, F., Law, R. and Smyth, N. (2018) 'Physical Fitness and Prior Physical Activity are Both Associated with Less Cortisol Secretion during Psychosocial Stress', *Anxiety, Stress, & Coping*, 31(2), pp. 135–145.

9

Coping with online assessment

Students have a love-hate relationship with assignments and exams. They know they need to be assessed so that they can be recognised for their knowledge and understanding. However, they would rather not have to go through the fuss and bother of writing essays or sitting in exam halls. Lecturers feel their pain. After all, every lecturer will have written many essays and sat through lengthy exams themselves to gain their qualifications. Indeed, I obtained my first degree many years ago, yet I still recall my exams. One troubled me greatly. It was held in the last week of my three-year degree programme. It was a three-hour exam that had only one question. There was no choice, and we were expected to write an essay over that three hours in which we brought in every aspect of our studies. Worse still, this single essay was worth an entire 10 per cent of the degree marks. Thankfully, these days such pressurised assessment is not the norm. Indeed, you will find a wide variety of assessments in your studies. As an example, here is a list of the types of assessment that I currently use in the modules that I teach:

- Blogs
- Case study analysis

DOI: 10.4324/9781003259695-11

- Consultancy reports
- Essays
- Exams
- Forum discussions
- Group projects
- Multiple-choice tests
- Podcasts
- Portfolios
- Posters
- Presentations
- Quizzes
- Reflections
- Research reports
- Roleplays
- Study logs
- Tutorial discussions.

That's quite a wide variety of assessment methods – and I hope to continue to innovate with new ways of assessing students. Not every subject is amenable to a range of assessment types, of course. Plus, science and engineering courses, among others, will require some practical assessments as well. Even so, the days of just having mid-term essays and end-of-term exams as the only form of assessment are pretty much over for today's students; and rightly so. This means that if you have a fear of exams or do not like writing essays, there will be other kinds of assessment in which you will be able to shine.

The move to online studying is a help for students. Gone are those cold and draughty exam halls because you will take your exams online. No longer will you have to wait outside an exam room, with everyone around you feeling nervous, making you more anxious than necessary. I remember waiting outside an exam room on a dreary cold winter morning, minding my own business when a couple of students near me started saying how they were worried about the exam. They said they didn't want a particular topic to come up as it was difficult. But they were sure it would be one of the questions as it hadn't been covered for the past few years. I, too, was worried about that subject. However, I had managed to eliminate it from my mind – until those students near me started talking about it. My anxiety levels shot up, which is not good as you are about to walk into the exam hall. For online exams, there is none of that. You can't be "infected" by the anxiety of those around you.

Another advantage of being an online student is that lecturers have to be more innovative with their assessments. This is because it's not as easy to do some group exercises that might have typically formed part of a course assessment. That's feasible when everyone is in the same classroom together, but not straightforward when all the students are studying separately at a distance to the university. In-class tests often occur during a module, for instance, and they are easier to arrange when everyone is in the same room. Universities also have concerns that online students may be more prone to cheating than those on campus. So, this is leading to innovative assessments for those studying online. Altogether, these factors mean that for anyone studying online, the assessment methods are likely to be more varied than has been the case traditionally.

Even so, assessment can be troubling for students. It can lead to anxiety, and this, in turn, can reduce your performance. Indeed, there is evidence that anxiety for assessments leads to lower results (Woldeab and Brothen, 2019). There appears to be a myth amongst many students that being anxious about tests and exams is good. It isn't; anxiety reduces your ability to perform at your best. So, if you want to gain the best possible marks for all of your assignments and exams, you need to ensure that your anxiety levels are low.

▶ REDUCING ANXIETY FOR ASSESSMENTS

The first step in reducing assessment or exam anxiety is knowing what is expected so that you can prepare. In the classic book *How to Pass Exams*, the author, Fred Orr, provides a clear guide on relaxing and avoiding anxiety (Orr, 2020). However, he warns that one of the reasons for nervousness is because preparation is left too late. Indeed, I can testify to this with my experience of students. Each term, I post the assessment in Week 1 on the VLE. That means that students can see what is expected of them in terms of assessment before they start studying. They know what they have to think about over the following weeks. Yet, every term, around a week before the assignment is due to be submitted, I'll get students calling into my office to ask when will I be posting the instructions for the assignment. I have to tell them that the instructions have been online on the VLE for the previous couple of months. Some students appear to only think about the assessment when it is almost the date for submission. I also teach at the Open University, and on their modules, all the assignments for the year ahead are available for students from day one of the course. That means these students know what they have to think about for an assignment that might not be required for six or nine months ahead. However, some students tell me that they "don't want to look" as assignments scare them. The problem with that approach is that they have lost the opportunity to prepare properly by the time they get to the assessment.

> **QUICK TIP:** *Take time to prepare thoroughly and understand precisely what is required for each assessment as soon as the information becomes available.*

For online students, there are two key areas of preparation:

1. Understand what the assignment is asking you to do; what do you have to provide?
2. Understand the technical requirements, such as file type and size.

Time management for assessments

Managing your time effectively has a significant impact on your anxiety levels. For example, a study of nursing students in China found that when they were given training in time management techniques, their anxiety levels fell (Zhang et al., 2021). Other research has shown that when students feel they are managing their time well, their performance in assessments improves (Adams and Blair, 2019). Indeed, this study showed that this was more important than other factors such as age, gender, entrance qualifications, and the number of semesters of being a student. It is an indication that time management is fundamental to preparation for assessments.

One problem with being an online student is that it is much easier to avoid time management than is the case for those students on campus. Studying alone, at a distance, means you can be more easily distracted, and you also do not have the encouragement of other students around you. It's all too easy to stay under the duvet and watch Netflix instead of getting on with work on planning your assignment. As a result, online students must get to grips with time management. When you manage your time well, you will feel less anxious, and that, in turn, will help you gain better marks in assignments and exams.

The late American psychologist, Professor Steven Covey, established a method of time management in the late 1980s and early 1990s that has since become a gold standard method. It is the basis of many time management systems. In his book about time management, *First Things First*, Professor Covey explained that there are only two elements to a task that we need to consider (Covey, 1994). The first of these is the urgency of the item – how soon does it need to be completed? The second is whether the item is important or not.

- If an item is neither urgent nor important, frankly, you can forget it.
- If an item is urgent but it is not important that you do it, then you can delegate it. Get someone else to do it.
- If an item is not urgent, but it is important you do it, then stick it in your diary for a future date.
- If an item is both urgent and important, then you need to get on with it. You need to do it.

Some time management trainers call this the "Four D" method of managing your tasks.

- Do it – if it is urgent and important
- Diarise it – if it is not urgent, but it is important
- Delegate it – if it is urgent but not important
- Dump it – if it is neither urgent nor important.

Some examples might help explain these options.

Let's imagine you have been told about an assignment a couple of months ahead. It is not urgent that you do this work, but it is important. So that's a "diarise it" item. Put some appointments in your diary to deal with the required work over the coming weeks.

If you have forgotten to check on what assignment work you need to do and have suddenly discovered the instructions, that has become both urgent and important. That's a "do it" item. You need to get on with it as soon as possible.

You could have been sent seen a newsletter in your email inbox that may have helpful information that could be used for the assignment. However, you are not sure, and you will need to read it all to see if there is something valuable. That is neither urgent nor important. You can just forget about it; "dump it".

Finally, one of your study buddies has contacted you to ask you if you have any information on one of the topics being studied. You don't have the information required, though you could find it. Instead, "delegate it" by suggesting another student for your buddy to contact.

The most important of these items is the "diarise it" option. This avoids doing urgent work and allows you to take a more relaxed approach to your studies. Instead of doing all the reading in a rush before the assignment is due, put non-urgent but important work in the diary, such as reading the textbook, this will smooth out your preparation for your assignments, which, in turn, will reduce anxiety. Then, as mentioned earlier, with reduced worry about your assessments, you will get higher marks.

▶ PREPARING YOUR ASSESSMENT ENVIRONMENT

If you were to take an exam on campus, you would have no control over the environment. The room is set up by the university authorities; even your seat is allocated to you. There is no choice as to where you sit. However, when you are doing any kind of assessment as an online distance study student, you have several options for where you will do the work. You can take exams in bed in the middle of the night if you wish, though I would not advise it.

You will want to be comfortable when writing an assignment. This means considering your study room and making sure that it will work well for you to help you gain those higher marks. In Chapter 2, you will have read about preparing your room for online study. However, when it comes to working on assignments, there are some other factors you need to consider.

Concentrating on the task at hand and getting the maximum possible marks is the principal requirement. This means taking a look at your study room and removing any distractions. Set aside books, notes, or other materials that do not relate to the assignment at hand. They may be needed for a future assignment, but if they are around you, they will distract you, reducing the potential for your marks.

With your electronic files, get everything you will need for the assignment into one folder or directory. This will stop you from being distracted by other work on other areas of study that you stumble across as you travel around your computer files. Remember, your computer filing system is part of your study environment. So, getting that into the appropriate organised state is crucial if you want to minimise distractions and stay focused on the assignment.

There is also one other aspect of computing you need to consider, and that is broadband access and bandwidth. You will want to make sure that when you are due to upload the assignment to the university's VLE that you are going to have enough Internet access. It's a regular occurrence for lecturers to get requests for extensions from students who have tried to upload their assignments at the required time, only to find they cannot do so. They have run out of data on their mobile device, for example. Or their WiFi is overloaded as everyone else in the house is using it at the same time. I do not give extensions in these situations, and I can't imagine many universities doing so. It is your responsibility to make sure that you have the technical capability to upload your files when required. If that means buying more data on your mobile package or asking others in the house to stop using their devices for five minutes, then so be it.

> QUICK TIP: *Make sure you will be able to upload your assignment on time and that you will have enough data allowance to do so.*

There is one other aspect of planning your environment for assignments: ensuring that everyone else in the household knows what you are doing. You need to focus on the work and get the best marks, so ask them to avoid distracting you. Parents, especially, need to know that you do not need constant interruptions asking if you are OK or need a cup of tea.

▶ HANDLING ONLINE FORMATIVE ASSESSMENTS

A formative assessment is the kind of assignment that helps check your progress. Sometimes this will be a simple quiz that allows you to see whether you have grasped particular facts, concepts, or ideas. Such quizzes are not marked and do not count towards your degree. They are tests that enable you to check your own progress. Another kind of formative assessment is a test that is "peer marked". This is where you complete the test, and another student will mark it. You then get the chance to also mark a different student's work. This kind of test helps you to see where others go wrong, and helping them put it right strengthens your understanding of the topic. Sometimes, though, formative assessments do count towards your module marks and your degree result. These assessments can include a mid-term essay, for example. You are marked by your lecturer, and you are given feedback about what you did well and what you could improve to gain higher marks. You can then use this feedback in the final assessment for the module, such as in the exam, so that you can improve your overall marks.

You are likely to see more online formative assessments than is commonplace for students on campus at traditional universities. This is because lecturers are realising the value of regular online tests for students learning at a distance. For example, research from Belgium shows that increasing the amount of testing for online students can help them avoid procrastination (Blondeel, Everaert and Opdecam, 2021). Other studies have found that students like online testing as it helps them consolidate what they have been learning (Shraim, 2019). There are many other recent studies all showing the value of regular testing for online students. This doesn't happen so much with face-to-face studying because students can more easily check their progress in class by speaking with the lecturer and asking questions. Online students have fewer opportunities to do this, so regular formative testing is a suitable replacement. As a result, you could well face tests and assessments regularly. Rather than see this as some kind of hindrance, it is designed to support you and help you so that you can increase your knowledge and understanding. Having said this, many formative assessments are not compulsory. They are tests and quizzes to help you monitor your own learning progress. This can mean that students often miss out the online tests as they see them as something of a waste of time and effort. Yet they are really going to help you improve, so it is worthwhile setting aside time to do them.

> QUICK TIP: Even if an online test is not compulsory, it is worthwhile doing it because it will help consolidate your learning, thereby improving your knowledge and understanding.

▶ HANDLING ONLINE SUMMATIVE ASSIGNMENTS

A summative assignment is where you are assessed on the sum total of your learning on the module. Each module at university has "learning outcomes". These are the things you are expected to be able to have achieved by the end of the course. The summative assessment is designed to check whether you have achieved those learning outcomes. Online, you may be asked to provide essays, reports, presentations, and various written, video, or audio materials. Because these assignments count towards your degree, it is essential you check the precise digital requirements. Submitting the wrong kind of file is going to stop you from getting the marks you deserve.

> QUICK TIP: Check the precise requirements for the kinds of files you need to upload for summative assignments. If you upload an incorrect type of file, you could lose marks or miss out on marks entirely.

There is an advantage for online students with assessments that take place over the web. Feedback provided by lecturers tends to be more extensive. Furthermore, it is easier for students to access. It is typed and linked to specific elements of the assignment submitted. However, for paper-based assignments on campus, there may be some scribbled comments at the end. Quite apart from the difficulty of reading the lecturer's handwriting, the comments are not always easily connected to specific elements of the assignment.

As a result, students like the way in which online assessments provide more easily accessible and more in-depth feedback than paper-based assignments (Al-Qdah and Ababneh, 2017).

However, there is a problem with this. The summative assignment will provide you with extensive feedback. You are not likely to be interested in it, though, because you will have completed that module and moved on to the next one. The feedback you get from lecturers is not always subject-specific. Much of the feedback will be about the way you have written things, the structure of the assignment, or the approach you took. These are general areas of academic work which could be applied to almost any other module you are likely to study. As a result, even though feedback on summative assessments will reach you after moving on from that subject, it is worth reading and considering. Some students have a "feedback book". This is a notebook that records all the feedback they have received on all their assignments. Whenever they are about to start work on a future assignment, they check their collated feedback from all their previous work. This helps them ensure they take into account the general feedback that can help them gain improved marks. You do not necessarily need to keep a feedback book. You could, for instance, copy all the feedback you receive on your assignments and paste it into a spreadsheet or document. You could then flick through that when new assessment time approaches. The fact is the feedback you get on each of your summative assignments will help you with your future assignments. So, make sure you take it into account.

> QUICK TIP: Keep a database of some kind, even a simple word processor document, of all the feedback you have received on previous assignments. You can then refer to this when a new assignment is due.

▶ TAKING ONLINE EXAMS

Even though you will be writing essays or reports, giving presentations, or delivering posters, you will still need to do exams. They have not been eliminated entirely. Online exams are not like those you have undertaken in an exam hall. Instead, the paper is provided online, and you have to submit your answers via the Internet. Universities have taken a variety of approaches to online examinations. However, two main ways have been used for online exams. These are:

1. Timed exams
2. Proctored exams.

Timed exams are where the exam paper is made available on the VLE at a specified time. You will then have a "window" of time in which to deliver your exam answers. Universities take a range of approaches to this. Some, for instance, will provide you with access to the exam paper for several days, allowing you to complete your work over a relatively long time. Other universities provide the exam paper for several days, but you have to provide your answers within a specified number of hours from the moment you download the paper. Some universities will provide the exam paper at a specific time and force you to complete the exam in a particular number of hours from the moment that paper is published online.

Proctored exams are where specialist software is used in place of an invigilator. When you have taken exams in the "real world", you will have had several invigilators in the exam hall. These are usually people who have no knowledge of the subject of the exam. They are merely responsible for ensuring all the exam protocols have taken place and that there is no cheating. In online exams, as there is no invigilator, it is easier to cheat. You can, for instance, look things up online or even go to your textbooks to find out information. Some universities adopt exam "proctoring", an electronic invigilation system, to avoid this happening. There is a variety of different methods of proctored exams. One, for instance, is where you are required to plug a USB device into your computer. This provides a different operating environment where all you can see is the exam paper and have access to something like Microsoft Word to complete your answers. The USB device prevents access to the Internet, so you can't look things up. However, universities are aware that you could use these USB devices on one laptop but still look things up using your mobile phone or have a physical textbook open on your desk. To avoid this, some proctoring software will take pictures of you working on a regular basis. If you have used your mobile phone to check something or flicked through the pages of a textbook, there will be a photo of you doing that. Another form of proctoring is where your webcam is switched on, and a video is recorded of you completing the exam. There is also a form of proctoring software that switches on your webcam and allows a remote invigilator to "pop in" and see what you are doing. All of these systems are in place to help prevent cheating.

Having said all this, many universities are also wary of proctored exams. There are issues with accessibility for disabled students, for example. They may not be able to use the proctoring software or may not have access to special programs if they are blind or dyslexic, for example. This is clearly unfair and is discriminatory. Also, proctored exams cost more money and take more time to organise. This is another reason why some universities do not like this kind of online exam there are concerns with privacy by taking images or videos of the home settings of students. However, there is another particular problem that universities are grappling with. Studies have shown that students perform worse in proctored exams than in similar exams without proctoring (Daffin and Jones, 2018). This may be due to the difficulties with using the software itself or feeling under pressure as though you are constantly being watched via the webcam. An alternative explanation is that the systems prevent students from cheating and that the higher marks obtained in other forms of online exams merely show the higher level of using textbooks and looking things up online. The result of all this confusion is that some universities do not like proctored exams, whereas others prefer them. Indeed, you can find fans of exam proctoring in one faculty at a university, with another faculty at the same university set against the use of proctored exams. Therefore, you may be asked to take a proctored exam, or you may never encounter one. It is not predictable.

> QUICK TIP: Check with your lecturers in advance if you will
> need to take a proctored exam. That way, you can ensure you
> are prepared.

If you are asked to take a proctored exam, there are some things
you should do beforehand. First, back up your computer. There
should not be any problems with the software used, but it is better
to be safe rather than sorry. Second, check your system has the
minimum requirements to allow the proctoring system to work.
You might need extra memory, for example, or you might need
a USB adaptor. Your university will let you know the specific requirements. However, make sure you sort out what is necessary in
advance of the exam. You do not want any added stress. You will
also want to ensure that the room where you take the exam does
not have anything visible you would not wish anyone else to see.
Sometimes students have potentially embarrassing items, such as
wall posters, which you would not want to be visible to anyone
checking the images or watching you via the webcam. In online
classes, students will often use the "Blur background" feature of
programs like Zoom or Microsoft Teams to avoid any embarrassing items being seen on screen. However, in online proctored exams, blurring is not allowed, and hence you may wish to remove
those embarrassing objects from view.

Practical steps for online exams

Whether your exam is timed or proctored, you need to be ready
in advance. You may not be allowed your mobile phone, for example. However, many students will use their smartphones as
their alarm clocks. Given that the exam is timed, you will need
a visible clock nearby. In traditional exam halls, there are usually several clocks. They are there so you can check your timings
for completing each question. You still need to be aware of the
timings for your answers in online exams. However, unless you

organise a clock, you could end up not completing the exam before the time is up. This is particularly important if you are prevented from using your mobile phone. It is also worth noting that smartwatches are banned from many exams because they could be used to access the Internet or have stored notes on them. Ultimately, a simple clock is all you need.

You also need to be sure that any battery-operated items, like a wireless mouse or keyboard, have new batteries or have been fully charged up. Otherwise, you could find yourself mid-exam without a keyboard or mouse. It may be a simple matter of swapping batteries. However, you do not want to do this mid-exam, adding to the stress and taking a few minutes. It may not be much time, but it will alter your concentration and disturb your focus. Plus, you don't want to find out halfway through an exam that you don't have any replacement batteries for your keyboard, and you need to go on a shopping expedition to find some.

If it is an "open book" exam, you will be allowed access to textbooks and your notes. In this instance, you will need to ensure you have everything at hand. Like preparing for an assignment, it would be a good idea to collect all of the necessary information in one folder or directory on your computer so that you do not waste time trying to find things during the exam.

QUICK TIP: *Make sure your computer is set up and ready for taking an exam well in advance. Otherwise, you will waste time on the day of the exam, increasing your stress.*

Submitting an online exam

The precise method of submitting an online exam will vary depending upon the process decided by your faculty or university. Make sure you check precisely what is required; otherwise, you could end up in difficulty. The critical information that you need to be confident you have correct includes:

- The date and time you are required to submit
- The kind of file that is needed (for example, do you need to submit a word processor document or a PDF file?)
- The maximum file size allowed
- The portal or link through which you should submit your exam paper.

Over the past couple of years, I have set and marked several online exams. Each time, some students submit late, send in the wrong kind of file, cannot submit because their file is too big, or send an email in a panic because they can't find the link to submit their paper. Avoid being stressed out by such factors by making sure you know exactly what to do in advance.

One other problem with exam file submission is sending an incorrect file. Each time I have set an online exam, I get files that are irrelevant and have nothing to do with the exam topic. As yet, no student has submitted anything embarrassing. However, I have received old assignments, notes on other subjects, and even exam papers for a different exam. This is because, in a rush towards the end of the exam time, students submit a file quickly and select the wrong one. You need to be more organised. Make sure your file has the correct name. Indeed, some examiners will request specific naming conventions, such as your student ID followed by the module name and exam date. Others will not have any naming conventions for the file, so you will need to save it with a recognisable and specific name. Just calling it "exam" doesn't do you any favours. The chances are you will have other files on your computer called "exam" if you do that. That makes it easy to submit the wrong one.

> **QUICK TIP:** If you are not told how to name your exam files, set up your own naming convention so that you do not submit the wrong paper.

▶ HOW TO AVOID BEING ACCUSED OF PLAGIARISM

Plagiarism is the use of someone else's work as though it were your own. It is a form of cheating because even if your work contains a small amount of plagiarism, the essay, for instance, is not entirely your own work. Yet you could be marked as though it were your own work. This would mean you were obtaining credit fraudulently because some of the marks would inevitably reflect the work done by someone else, not you. The fact is, though, the vast majority of plagiarism is unintentional. Only a small proportion of students deliberately set out to deceive and cheat their way to good results. However, significant numbers of students end up facing an "Academic Misconduct" investigation because it appears they have cheated when they actually did not do so. These students unintentionally copied material. However, the result is still the same; not everything in their assignment is their own work. So, why should they be credited for it?

For online students, the opportunity to cheat, even unintentionally, is often easier than for traditional campus-based students. On campus, students will often be seen in the library with a textbook and a notepad. Those studying online, though, may just have several tabs open on their browser and just copy and paste material into their digital notetaking system. It's easier to do this when you are entirely online than for students who are on campus. The result of this way of working, though, is that an online student's digital notetaking files can be full of copied material. When the student completes an assignment using their "notes", they forget where the original material came from. They assume it is their own notes and copy what they believe is their own work into the assignment when it is someone else's material.

Various studies of online students and the degree of cheating appear to provide conflicting results. Some studies point towards a higher level of plagiarism amongst online students than those on campus. However, other research suggests there is no more cheating with online students than there has ever been with traditional studying. As a result, it isn't yet clear if those who study online are more likely to want to cheat. The issue appears to be the opportunity to inadvertently cheat is greater for online students than traditional students. As a result, there is a higher chance that online students will face accusations of Academic Misconduct, even though there is no deliberate attempt to deceive amongst the majority of students learning at a distance.

You do not want an Academic Misconduct investigation

Universities use plagiarism detection software, such as Turnitin, Copyleaks, or Copycatch. These can detect copying from websites and from work submitted by students in other universities around the world. These plagiarism detectors have massive databases and artificial intelligence, which can spot even small amounts of copying from elsewhere. All of your work will inevitably go through at least one of these detection systems, and should elements of your assignment or your exam be found to be copied, you could be called in for an Academic Misconduct investigation. In this, you will be questioned by someone other than your lecturer and asked to explain how the material was copied. You may have to face a panel interview, or the Academic Misconduct official will just consider the evidence provided by Turnitin, for example. Apart from the stress of not knowing what will happen, several problems can arise from even inadvertent copying. Some of the options that universities select include:

- Reduced marks for the assignment, taking into account the amount copied
- The need to resubmit the assignment, but only for marks that are capped at the pass mark
- A score of zero for the assignment
- The need to resit the entire module and complete new assignments

- A score of zero for the entire module with no opportunity to resit
- A need to resit the entire semester
- A need to resit the entire year
- Expulsion from the university.

As you can see, the typical penalties range from mild to severe. For cases of small amounts of unintentional copying, the typical penalty would be reduced marks. You don't want that to happen, so avoiding unintentional copying is essential. However, there is another important reason. Many universities record instances of Academic Misconduct on your "Academic Transcript". This is a document that shows all of your marks and achievements for each of your individual modules. This document is sometimes requested by potential employers or other universities if you go on to do another degree. You certainly do not wish employers, for example, to see that you were accused of cheating in your degree. That does not create the right impression. Hence, it is not only crucial for the marks on your module to avoid plagiarism, but it is also of fundamental importance to your future career prospects.

Take proper notes

I have investigated many students for potential breaches of academic conduct, and in most instances, the issue comes down to poor notetaking. Students appear to have no way of knowing where they obtained the information they have in their notes. As a result, they can mistakenly think the work is their own when it is actually copied. They only discover this when Turnitin or Copyleaks, for instance, has identified the original source. To avoid plagiarism, make sure you follow the guidance in Chapter 4 on taking notes. Also, it is good practice to rewrite your own notes. Review your notes and then rewrite them. This helps consolidate what you have learned, but it also reduces the chances of using copied material as you will have rewritten anything you copied inadvertently.

Avoid "Essay Mills"

There are several "Essay Mills" online. These are websites that provide examples of essays, often from former students. Many of these sites purport to just allow students to share examples of essays so that others can get helpful ideas. The problem is that users of the essay mill websites have no knowledge of whether those example essays achieved high marks. You may well find that what looks like a good essay was actually a failed assignment. In addition, many essay mills offer assignment writing services. For a small sum of money, someone else will write your essay for you. It sounds like a great idea, except, of course, it is cheating. The essay that people present from essay mills is not their own work. It is ghost-written for them, which is fraudulent behaviour. Worse still for the students forking out money for these essay mills is that the writers of the assignments will often plagiarise anyway. As a result, the essay that the student did not write is picked up for plagiarism through something like Turnitin. That's a double penalty for the student because they have paid for an essay and have also been found to be cheating by copying. Some essay mills guarantee that the work they provide will be completely genuine and will not trigger plagiarism detection software. However, they forget that these essays will trigger the human detection of lecturers. We get to know our student's style and way of working. We can spot the difference between a student's usual work and an essay they have submitted, which is out of the ordinary for them. That alone can trigger an Academic Misconduct investigation. Furthermore, even if the assessments are marked anonymously, statistical software will demonstrate an out of range mark for a student once the anonymity is removed at the end of the marking period. This will then trigger a lecturer to look at the submitted work again, at which point anything suspicious for that student could be identified. As a result, paying for an essay to be written for you is a complete waste of money. Not only are you likely to be found out, but you are also cheating yourself. You will know that the marks you get, perhaps even the degree classification you receive, is not deserved. That's something you will need to live with for the rest of your life. Can you imagine telling your children you cheated to get a degree? For online students, essay mills are just a click away. Sometimes, it is a good idea not to click.

Understand the rules about academic integrity

For the majority of Academic Misconduct investigations that I have conducted, a student will say to me at some point, "but I provided a reference". There is a mistaken belief among many students that it is perfectly acceptable to copy material as long as the source is referenced. That is simply not true. The words within your text, though cited from somewhere else, are not your words. You are being marked on your knowledge and understanding, not that of the textbook's authors, for instance.

Another common misconception is that if the material is in quotation marks, it isn't plagiarism. Technically, as long as there is a reference for quoted material, you are indicating that the text is not your own. So, it is not actually a case of cheating. However, students tend to use large chunks of quoted material. Indeed, in one instance I investigated, 75 per cent of the essay was quoted material. That meant only a quarter of the essay was written by the student themself. I asked if he only wanted a quarter of the marks. Quoting extensive amounts of material is poor academic practice, plus it doesn't avoid an Academic Misconduct investigation. So, it is better to ensure that everything is in your own words.

QUICK TIP: Don't make assumptions about what is or is not allowed in terms of copying material or using items from your sources. Instead, just put everything in your assignment entirely in your own words.

PRACTICAL TIPS

- **Prepare for assessments in advance.** Taking assignments and exams can be stressful. The sooner you prepare for all assessments, the less anxiety you will suffer. Check out every assignment as soon as you are told about it and find out precisely what you need to do.
- **Manage your time.** Poor time management is a significant factor in lower marks for students. There is a clear relationship between high marks and good time management. If you are aiming for high marks, managing your time is crucial. The "Four D" method of time management, of "Do it", "Diarise it", "Delegate it", or "Dump it", works well for students.
- **Get your assessment environment ready.** Make sure that you are writing assignments free of distractions. Get your family to understand you are doing something important and don't want to be interrupted. Ensure that your digital environment is organised with everything you need collecting into one folder or directory.
- **Take all the formative tests.** Online students will face several optional tests and quizzes. There is often a temptation to avoid them. However, these tests help consolidate your learning and lead to higher marks in the assignments and exams you will take at the end of the module.
- **Take care with assignment submissions.** You will lose marks in your assignments and exams if you do not submit correctly. Check the date you are required to submit, the kind of file you should send, and the maximum file sizes. Be sure to submit the correct file too.
- **Avoid accusations of plagiarism.** Use an effective notetaking system to avoid inadvertent copying. Don't fall into the trap of believing some of the myths that circulate, suggesting you can avoid being accused of plagiarism as long as you include a reference.

▶ REFERENCES

Adams, R.V. and Blair, E. (2019) 'Impact of Time Management Behaviors on Undergraduate Engineering Students' Performance', *SAGE Open*, 9(1).

Al-Qdah, M. and Ababneh, I. (2017) 'Comparing Online and Paper Exams: Performances and Perceptions of Saudi Students', *International Journal of Information and Education Technology*, 7(2), pp. 106–109.

Blondeel, E., Everaert, P. and Opdecam, E. (2021) 'Stimulating Higher Education Students to Use Online Formative Assessments: The Case of Two Mid-Term Take-Home Tests', *Assessment & Evaluation in Higher Education*, pp. 1–16.

Covey, S. (1994) *First Things First*. London: Simon & Schuster.

Daffin Jr., L.W. and Jones, A.A. (2018) 'Comparing Student Performance on Proctored and Non-Proctored Exams in Online Psychology Courses', *Online Learning*, 22(1). DOI: 10.24059/olj.v22i1.1079 (Accessed: 15 August 2021).

Orr, F. (2020) *How to Pass Exams*, 2nd edn. Abingdon: Routledge.

Shraim, K. (2019) 'Online Examination Practices in Higher Education Institutions: Learners' Perspectives', *Turkish Online Journal of Distance Education*, 20(4), pp. 185–196.

Woldeab, D. and Brothen, T. (2019) '21st Century Assessment: Online Proctoring, Test Anxiety, and Student Performance', *International Journal of e-Learning & Distance Education*, 34(1). Available at: https://eric.ed.gov/?id=EJ1227595 (Accessed: 31 October 2021).

Zhang, F., Liu, J., An, M. and Gu, H. (2021) 'The Effect of Time Management Training on Time Management and Anxiety among Nursing Undergraduates', *Psychology, Health & Medicine*, 26(9), pp. 1073–1078.

Part III

Coping online

10 Avoiding distractions

Students are always at risk of being distracted from their studies. It makes no difference whether you are studying online or face-to-face; there are plenty of things you can do as a student other than study. Indeed, in a face-to-face lecture recently, a student told me that she was tired and unable to concentrate. She wanted me to explain a theory again, as she felt she hadn't quite "got it". I asked why she was so tired, and she said that it was because she didn't finish the work for class until 5:00 am. Naturally, I wondered why she had left it so late. It transpired that while she was cooking dinner the evening before, some of her housemates suggested a trip out. She had told them she was due to complete some work, so she could not go. But then she relented and said that she would do the work when they got back. Apparently, one of her mates said that she was unlikely to do it despite her promises to get on with the work immediately after returning. Of course, when she got back from the outing, she went straight to bed, ignoring the work. Then she woke up in a mild panic at 4:00 am when she suddenly remembered she had not completed the classwork. So, she had to

DOI: 10.4324/9781003259695-13

get up and do the work ready for when she met me in the lecture just a few hours later.

This is typical student behaviour. There are sudden opportunities to do things you haven't planned. The spontaneity of student life is something that university students love. Indeed, it is part of being a student. Lecturers used to be students themselves, so we understand the distractions that exist for anyone studying on campus. Quite apart from the Student Union bar, there are all sorts of clubs and societies that have meetings and events. Plus, there are talks and seminars organised by the university itself. As a campus-based university student, you are never short of anything to do.

Therefore, it might seem that being an online student means you will not get distracted anywhere near as much. However, that line of thinking ignores the many distractions there are at home if that is where you study. There's the local pub, rather than the Student Union, but there are also all your school friends to hang out with. Then there are the family pets to look after before you even think about spending time with your siblings, chatting to the neighbours, or watching that local sports team you love so much. There are plenty of distractions from studying, even if you are not on campus. Research conducted by psychologists in Greece shows that distractions at home are a real problem for those studying online (Kostaki and Karayianni, 2021).

Worse still, for those studying online, there are all the distractions of the Internet within easy reach. For face-to-face students sitting in lecture theatres or classrooms, being distracted by the Internet is less likely as they are busily engaged with what is happening in the room (or should be ...!). For online students, though, all of their work is on the Internet. Hence, they get even more distracted. Even though students on campus complain about being distracted by the various and spontaneous activities, those studying entirely online probably have a much more challenging time dealing with the variety of distractions that come their way.

▶ THE FUNDAMENTALS OF AVOIDING DISTRACTIONS

One of the main reasons we get distracted is that our subconscious brain reminds us of something we might have forgotten or missed out on. When your brain is comfortable that a task has been done, it does not trigger you with constant reminders.

One way of thinking about this is by considering brushing your teeth. Did you clean your teeth this morning? Of course, you did. You do it every morning, probably at roughly the same time each day. You don't need reminding because it is a routine. You have been brushing your teeth every morning ever since you were a small toddler. Because you have such a routine, your brain knows it does not need to interrupt you every now and then to ask, "Have you cleaned your teeth?" If you couldn't remember whether you had done it, you would rush to the bathroom and give them the once over. Later in the day, your brain will want to check again because it isn't sure. So, you would be distracted for a moment while you had to think, "Did I do them a couple of hours ago, or was that yesterday?" You would then think better to be safe, so you would rush to the bathroom once more.

Now let's think about any of your social media accounts. Do you, like tooth brushing, check into your social media account at roughly the same time every day? Have you been doing that for several years? You can probably see where this is heading, can't you? Without a routine for checking social media, your subconscious brain is not sure whether you have, in fact, logged in and checked the latest posts. So, it sends a message saying, "Check your social media". You oblige and then read a few posts before returning to your work. Later in the day, your brain isn't really sure, so it prompts you to check again. So it goes on throughout the day.

The reason you do not constantly go and brush your teeth several times a day is because your brain is safe in the knowledge you did so as a result of having a long-standing routine. Without a routine for checking social media or emails, your brain isn't sure. So, it triggers lots of reminders to keep checking.

The most important thing to do to reduce online distractions is to set up routines and make them a habit. Have times in the day that are your "email checking times", or have a daily "social media" time, for example. It doesn't matter when you do these tasks, but setting them up as routines will significantly impact your productivity as you will be less distracted by constant subconscious pushes to check something else online.

> **QUICK TIP:** Establish routines for checking emails and social media. Doing so will reduce distractions a great deal.

It is vital to do everything you can to minimise distractions while studying. Plenty of research demonstrates a link between a lack of focus on studying and lower marks in assignments and tests. One study, for example, showed that marks can drop by almost 40 per cent when students are distracted from their work (Blasiman, Larabee, and Fabry, 2018). It is therefore crucial that you do everything you can to minimise distractions. Setting up routines is an excellent first step.

▶ STAYING FOCUSED WHILE STUDYING ONLINE

The myriad distractions for online students means it can be challenging to remain focused for very long. In one research project that looked at how often students switch their focus, psychologists from California State University found that individuals changed what they were doing frequently. The researchers discovered that students only remained focused on a single task for up to six minutes (Rosen, Carrier, and Cheever, 2013). When I ask students about their online studies, they tell me similar things, pointing out that studying online is mentally draining due to constantly switching from one screen to the next. However, much of that switching of tasks is not part of the course being studied. It can be switching attention to a news website, for example, or to read the latest blog from an influencer. As one student said in answer to my questionnaire about studying online, "Internet distractions take away the continuity of learning".

The chopping and changing from one screen or program to another lies at the heart of being distracted while studying online. When you move to the web browser, for instance, to access the VLE, you inevitably "bump into" something else on that browser window, such as your latest emails or a news website you had been looking at earlier in the day. These elements can remove your focus and take you away from what you had intended to do.

QUICK TIP: *To avoid being distracted by other browser tabs, when you need to open something for studying, such as an ebook, or the VLE, open a new browser window, not a new tab. That way, there is nothing to distract you.*

Time blocking

One method of staying focused is known as "time blocking". This is a time management method favoured by several leading entrepreneurs. Bill Gates, the founder of Microsoft, is reported to use time blocking, as is Jack Dorsey, one of the founders of Twitter. Plus, Benjamin Franklin, one of the USA's founding fathers, demonstrated the concept of time blocking in his autobiography (Franklin, n.d.).

The notion of time blocking is straightforward. You block out a time in your diary for a specific kind of task, which is all you do during that time. So you might block out an hour for reading a textbook, an hour for watching lecture videos, and another hour for writing notes. In those blocks of time in your diary, you do nothing else. For example, you do not need to worry about watching videos while reading your textbook because you know there is a block of time in your diary when you will be doing that.

TODAY	
08:30	Emails and social media
09:00	Reading material on the VLE
09:30	
10:00	Online chat
10:30	Textbook reading
11:00	
11:30	
12:00	Lecture videos
12:30	
13:00	Lunch
13:30	Tutorial work
14:00	
14:30	
15:00	Assignment writing
15:30	
16:00	
16:30	
17:00	
17:30	Catching up with other students
18:00	Emails and social media

Figure 10.1 An example of time blocking

Otherwise, you would suddenly remember there's a lecture video to watch, and so you would stop reading the textbook, head over to YouTube, watch the video, and then probably forget you had to finish reading the chapter.

When you block out your time like this, you are much less likely to be distracted, and you become more productive. According to a paper aimed at academics who need to get more material published, the author pointed out that individuals who use time blocking are the most productive (Kwok, 2020). Time blocking is widespread within many businesses because it helps to improve staff productivity. That's because it enables them to be focused.

The Pomodoro Technique®

The Pomodoro Technique® is a time management system developed by the business consultant Francesco Cirillo when he was a student. He was reading a sociology textbook for an exam in his family home just north of Rome in 1987. He used a kitchen timer in the shape of a tomato to help him time his work with the book. That led him to discover that he worked best by staying focused for 25 minutes. He set his tomato-shaped timer to help him focus. The Italian for "tomato" is *pomodoro*, which is how the technique got its name. Nowadays, the Pomodoro Technique® is used by millions of people in businesses and universities worldwide. As Francesco Cirillo says in his book about the technique, he had no idea that the chief executive of a bank, amongst many others, would adopt the technique to keep board meetings focused (Cirillo, 2018).

The basis of the Pomodoro Technique® is dividing your time into 25-minute chunks and using a timing device to ensure you stick to it. For instance, you can use your mobile phone alarm clock, or you can get several apps that help achieve this. Or, you could even buy a tomato-shaped kitchen timer and go "old school". Research conducted at the Department of Educational Research at

Lancaster University into the use of the Pomodoro Technique®
by students produced some interesting findings (Usman, 2020).
The study found that the Pomodoro Technique® certainly did help
students improve their focus and their progress with studying.
However, there wasn't a consensus among the participants in the
research as to how the technique actually helped them. What the
research found was that students did need a little time to get used
to the technique. Once they got to grips with it, though, it clearly
did help. So, spending time understanding the Pomodoro Tech-
nique® appears to be worthwhile in helping you focus.

> **QUICK TIP: Find a way of focusing that works for you. Whether
> it's time blocking, the Pomodoro Technique®, or your own per-
> sonal method, focusing clearly helps improve your productivity
> and is linked to better marks.**

Switch off notifications

The digital world is full of "notifications". You get notified automatically whenever an email arrives, if someone sends you a message, or
if your computer has completed some background activity. You do
not need to know any of it. Hardly any of the notifications you get
are essential. However, these notifications constantly interrupt you,
preventing you from staying focused.

There is a good reason for these notifications. They ensure you increase your engagement with a variety of software such as email
programs or social media apps. The good reason, though, is not
good for you. Instead, these notifications are for the benefit of software companies and social media giants. That's because you get a
"beep", and you check what has arrived. This means you will enter
the app. This increase in traffic to the company's app allows them
to charge more for advertising and means you are more likely to see
such promotional material. The primary recipients of the benefits
of notifications are the software giants, not the users. Notifications
are mainly a money-making device. You are not making that money, so there is no reason to have them switched on.

The reason we like notifications is because of FOMO – the Fear Of Missing Out. We tend to think that we'll miss an important message or posting from someone. Students with high levels of FOMO tend to interact with the notifications more, which appears to affect the learning process (Rozgonjuk et al., 2019). However, as outlined earlier, your brain will not sense you are missing out once you establish a routine for checking emails and social media at the same time every day. Therefore, you can switch off all notifications on your mobile phone and on your computer safe in the knowledge that you will see any important messages or postings later in the day when your routine time for checking takes place. Switching off notifications means you will not get disturbed, your attention will not get switched, and you will be able to remain focused on your studies.

> QUICK TIP: *Switch off unnecessary notifications on your mobile devices and on your computer. They serve no useful purpose.*

There are some notifications you should keep switched on, though. These might include notifications from family members. Also, you will want to the notifications from your university switched on, otherwise, you will miss out on important information. Indeed, one of my students had all notifications switched off, including from the messaging service of our VLE. That meant he missed out on the message saying that the lecture had been moved to a different room. He arrived at the lecture theatre to find there was nobody there, so he wondered where everyone had gone to. If you don't keep university notifications switched on, you will miss out on important information.

Use background music

Having background music while studying can be a real help in maintaining focus. Research in Germany has found that when students have background music while studying, it can improve comprehension (Lehmann and Seufert, 2017). It appears to do this by increasing the "working memory capacity" of your brain. Effectively, that means you can hold more things in your temporary memory, enabling you to process more pieces of information. The German research showed that this effect happened for most people, except for individuals who already have low memory issues. So, it has been shown background music can help most students concentrate.

One way it might help students is by making them feel better and more positive while studying. Research among students in Hong Kong has demonstrated that fast tempo background music can improve mood (Hu, Li, and Kong, 2019). Clearly, if you are in a more positive mood, you are likely to find studying a better experience. However, you need to be sure to only use instrumental music. Research at the University of Tennessee found that lyrics in music while studying appear to distract students enough to reduce their performance (Oliver, Levy, and Baldwin, 2021).

> *QUICK TIP: Play some fast-paced instrumental music in the background, and you will feel better and will probably remain more focused on your studies.*

If you listen to background music through noise-cancelling headphones, you will also avoid being unnecessarily interrupted by members of your family while you are studying.

▶ AVOIDING INTERRUPTIONS AT HOME

Online students often study at home. This means they are prone to several potential interruptions. These can include siblings, parents, school friends, and neighbours. They see you "at home", which to them means you are not "at university". Except, of course, you are at university, just via the Internet. Because the people around you perceive you as being at home, they will find it easier to interrupt you and distract you from your work. In Chapter 2, you will have seen the need to establish ground rules. However, you can take some additional measures to help avoid being interrupted while you are studying.

One effective way of doing this is with a series of door signs. You can make these easily by printing out some signs. If you want to be artistic, you can use an online creative graphics program like Canva (www.canva.com). You could have a range of signs such as:

- Do not disturb
- Come back in 25 minutes
- Available in an hour
- Happy to chat for five minutes.

If you have one of these on your study room door, the rest of the household and visitors will know what to do. Signs that make it clear you cannot be interrupted or when you can be spoken with are helpful to the people around you. If they know, for instance, that you are "Available in an hour", they will not interrupt you. Parents, in particular, are prone to keep knocking on their children's doors and asking, "Everything OK?". That's a needless interruption that destroys your focus and slows down your studying. If your parents can see a sign saying "Come back in 25 minutes", they will only interrupt you when you want to be sociable. This will allow you to remain much more focused on your studies.

▶ USING APPS TO AVOID DISTRACTIONS

There are several ways in which you can use apps to help reduce the impact of distractions while studying. Staying focused is not always easy, especially when studying at home. However, there are several digital options available to you that can help you remain focused. They can also let you analyse your working pattern so that you can see what distracts you the most, and therefore be able to deal with that issue.

There are several apps that help with online distractions. One that will help you analyse your personal situation is called Rescue Time (www.rescuetime.com). This detects all of your computer and on-line activities and can prepare charts and graphs to show you how you are spending your time. Often, people think they have only spent "a few minutes" on their favourite social media site. The data collected by Rescue Time could show you that this is far from the case. Indeed, in test results that I was shown, people who said they had been on a social media site for three minutes turned out to have been there for around 18 minutes – six times longer than they thought. Published research shows that there is the poten-tial for time distortion when using social media (Turel, Brevers, and Bechara, 2018). So, Rescue Time can reveal just how much time you are spending on social media sites, for example. It could be significantly more than you think. According to data collected by the website We Are Social, we are now individually spending almost two and a half hours on social media every day (Kemp, 2021). That's a great deal of time out of your study day. Of course, this is an average figure, so there is a chance your social media usage is a lot less. Equally, it could be a great deal higher. Getting Rescue Time will help you find out. It will also show you your pat-tern of use. The app will help you see how frequently you "drop-in" and for how long; you could be surprised. Having this knowledge, though, enables you to see what issues need fixing and so you can work out what you need to do to remain focused. Rescue Time itself can help by allowing you to focus during particular periods, even blocking access to sites that could distract you during your study time.

There are also apps which work by switching off access to specific sites to help you to remain focused. Even if you decide to check a social media page, these blockers will prevent you from going there until a specific time has elapsed. These apps are collectively known as "distraction blockers", and you can find a list on the website I have created to accompany this book, https://studyingonline.tips.

QUICK TIP: Get an app to block distractions so that you can focus on your studies.

PRACTICAL TIPS

- **Establish routines.** If you set up (and stick to) regular routines for things like checking emails and social media accounts, your brain will not trigger constant checking. This will help prevent you from being distracted. Check your emails once in the morning and once in the evening, and that should be enough. Also, you won't miss out if you check your social media once a day.
- **Use time blocking.** You can stay much more focused on your work if you block out periods of time to do specific tasks. You might spend the mornings doing reading, for instance, and the afternoons writing. When you block out timeslots in your calendar for specific activities, you become more productive. Plus, you avoid trying to multitask as you know the other tasks will get done as they are in the diary.
- **Study in short bursts.** Study for short periods of time, around 25 minutes long. Using The Pomodoro Technique® will allow you to study efficiently and avoid distractions as you can "save" the potential interruptions until after the 25-minute study session.
- **Switch off notifications.** You don't need to be notified of every email or social media post. Switch off notifications on your phone and on your computer, except for the ones that are sent by the university which are essential.
- **Use background music.** Get some fast-paced instrumental music and listen to it through noise-cancelling headphones while you are studying. You will find studying more enjoyable, and you will not be interrupted by your family. They may try, but you won't hear them. Also, listening to instrumental music helps with your memory capacity.
- **Get some door signs.** Get a range of door signs that explain to your family when you can and cannot be interrupted. This will help minimise or eliminate family interruptions when studying at home.
- **Use apps.** Several apps can block out digital distractions. It's a good idea to use these so that you can remain focused on your studies.

▶ REFERENCES

Blasiman, R.N., Larabee, D. and Fabry, D. (2018) 'Distracted Students: A Comparison of Multiple Types of Distractions on Learning in Online Lectures', *Scholarship of Teaching and Learning in Psychology*, 4(4), pp. 222–230.

Cirillo, F. (2018) *The Pomodoro Technique*®: *The Life-Changing Time-Management System*. London: Virgin Books.

Franklin, B. (n.d.) *The Autobiography of Benjamin Franklin*. Available at: https://standardebooks.org/ebooks/benjamin-franklin/the-autobi ography-of-benjamin-franklin (Accessed: 2 November 2021).

Hu, X., Li, F. and Kong, R. (2019) 'Can Background Music Facilitate Learning? Preliminary Results on Reading Comprehension', in *Proceedings of the 9th International Conference on Learning Analytics & Knowledge*, pp. 101–105. New York: ACM Press. DOI: 10.1145/3303772.3303839 (Accessed: 15 August 2021).

Kemp, S. (2021) 'Digital 2021: The Latest Insights into the "State of Digital"', We Are Social USA. Available at: https://wearesocial.com/us/blog/2021/01/digital-2021-the-latest-insights-into-the-state-of-digital (Accessed: 4 November 2021).

Kostaki, D. and Karayianni, I. (2021) 'Houston, We Have a Pandemic: Technical Difficulties, Distractions and Online Student Engagement'. Available at: www.researchgate.net/publication/349841086_Houston_ we_Have_a_Pandemic_Technical_Difficulties_Distractions_and_ Online_Student_Engagement (Accessed 2 November 2021).

Kwok, R. (2020) 'You Can Get That Paper, Thesis or Grant Written — With a Little Help', *Nature*, 580(7801), pp. 151–153.

Lehmann, J.A.M. and Seufert, T. (2017) 'The Influence of Background Music on Learning in the Light of Different Theoretical Perspectives and the Role of Working Memory Capacity', *Frontiers in Psychology*, 8, p. 1902.

Oliver, M.D., Levy, J.J. and Baldwin, D.R. (2021) 'Examining the Effects of Musical Type and Intensity in Performing the Flanker Task: A Test of Attentional Control Theory Applied to Non-Emotional Distractions', *Psychology of Music*, 49(4), pp. 1017–1026.

Rosen, L.D., Carrier, L.M. and Cheever, N.A. (2013) 'Facebook and Texting Made Me Do It: Media-Induced Task-Switching While Studying', *Computers in Human Behavior*, 29(3), pp. 948–958.

Rozgonjuk, D., Elhai, J.D., Ryan, T. and Scott, G.G. (2019) 'Fear of Missing Out is Associated with Disrupted Activities from Receiving Smartphone Notifications and Surface Learning in College Students', *Computers & Education*, 140, p. 103590.

Turel, O., Brevers, D. and Bechara, A. (2018) 'Time Distortion When Users At-Risk for Social Media Addiction Engage in Non-Social Media Tasks', *Journal of Psychiatric Research*, 97, pp. 84–88.

Usman, S.A. (2020) 'Using the Pomodoro Technique® to Help Undergraduate Students Better Manage Technology-Based Multitasking during Independent Study: A Design-Based Research Investigation', PhD. Lancaster: Lancaster University. Available at: https://eprints.lancs.ac.uk/id/eprint/153513/1/2020usmanphd.pdf (Accessed: 15 August 2021).

Online
well-being

There are two significant differences between face-to-face study-ing on campus and being an online student. The first is that cam-pus studying involves a great deal of walking. On a typical day on campus, I can do about 15,000 steps, according to the step counter on my smartphone. I have to walk from the car park to my office. Then I may need to walk to a lecture theatre on the other side of campus before walking back to my office and then off out to another building for a tutorial. This constant moving around the campus, walking down corridors to meetings and so on means that we are active. Campus students are much like lecturers, wan-dering from room to room, from one side of campus to the other. However, online students only have to go from their bed to their desk. At home, a student studying online could find themselves doing fewer than 100 steps a day, which is drastically different from the 15,000 I might do each day on campus. Studying online makes you somewhat static and largely sedentary.

The second issue with online study is the use of the computer it-self. Those who are studying online do everything through their computer screen. You can find yourself sitting for hours hunched

DOI: 10.4324/9781003259695-14

over your laptop, staring at the monitor. This can affect your eyesight and your muscles. Students on campus are constantly changing the focus of what they look at. They might look at a large screen in a lecture theatre, then their notebook as they make notes. They might turn to people around them when asked to discuss something. Even sitting still in a lecture theatre tends to involve changes in position and visual focus. For online students that does not happen. Studying online, therefore, can affect your eyes and muscles in ways that do not happen for those taking part in traditional face-to-face learning.

▶ SITTING AT YOUR COMPUTER

Sitting at your computer for several hours is not good for your body. Your muscles become stiff, and they ache. Being sedentary can also lead to tiredness, circulatory problems, and an increase in your chance of getting diabetes (Park et al., 2020). It can even reduce the level of your sex hormones, increase the chances of depression, and cause "cognitive impairment", the inability to think straight. According to the World Health Organization, being sedentary is a leading "killer" and causes two million deaths a year (World Health Organization, 2002). If you spend three years studying online, not moving much beyond the computer, you are sowing the seeds of trouble for your future health.

> **QUICK TIP:** *Take regular breaks from your computer. Get up and move about.*

Research has shown that discomfort in students is associated with the length of time they are using their computers (Osama, Ali, and Malik, 2018). According to the Health and Safety Executive, it is better to have a five- to ten-minute break every hour than longer breaks after a couple of hours (Health and Safety Executive, n.d.).

There are several advantages to taking frequent breaks. Not only will your muscles get a chance to move, relax, and reduce tension, but there are other benefits of taking frequent breaks. Studies have shown that regular breaks from working at a computer can:

- Improve your ability to concentrate
- Help your memory
- Enable you to be more focused
- Make you more creative
- Raise motivation
- Increase productivity
- Have a positive effect on your body's chemistry.

Far from disturbing your work, frequent breaks make significant improvements. Furthermore, regular breaks reduce your level of tiredness (Pragier, 1986). Sitting still at your computer for hours at a time should be avoided. If you were to use the Pomodoro Technique® discussed in Chapter 10, you could ensure you took a break after each 25-minute study period.

Check your posture

Seeing students hunched over their computers is a common sight in coffee bars and campus study rooms. However, these students will also move about, stop and chat with friends, or get up after a while and head off to a lecture theatre. Studying online means you can remain hunched over your computer for much more extended time periods. Clearly, taking breaks will help. So too will adopting a good posture while at your computer. Ideally, you will have a screen that is at the same level as your eyes when sitting down. If you have a laptop, this will mean getting a riser to raise the device to be at a better height. That way, you can avoid stooping and bending, which can lead to muscular problems in your neck, shoulders, and back. Research that compared the use of a laptop on a desk, a special lap desk, or just on the lap showed that having the computer on a desk was the best option (Asundi et al., 2010). If you must use your laptop on your lap, get one of those special lap desks that support the computer. Having your laptop on your lap appears to create more muscle problems.

Use a sit-stand desk

As explained in Chapter 2, there has been increasing interest in recent years in the concept of sit-stand desks. These are desks that can be raised and lowered. This means you can sit at them as a standard desk or raise them and stand up to use them. The cheaper desks are mechanical, and you wind them up or down. There are also electrically operated sit-stand desks that you raise or lower with the press of a button. There are even sophisticated sit-stand desks that include USB connectors, passive charging options for mobile phones, and several memory functions so the desk can be raised to a variety of heights to suit different users. Research has shown a range of benefits when using sit-stand desks. Compared with just sitting at a desk, sit-stand desks help reduce discomfort, lower overall fatigue, and cut down on tiredness (Kowalsky et al., 2018).

However, sit-stand desks can be expensive. Even the mechanical wind-up desks can cost three or four times the price of a standard desk. The sophisticated electronic desks can cost ten times as much as an ordinary desk. Of course, you will be using the desk for at least three years, so you will get value from it. Even so, the costs can be off-putting for students unless the bank of mum and dad has plenty of spare cash. An alternative to a sit-stand desk is an adaptor that you place on top of a standard desk. You can place your computer screen and keyboard on this and then raise it when you want to stand up to work. Such devices cost considerably less than a full sit-stand desk but can provide the same benefits as they allow you to work standing up or sitting down, depending on your requirements. Even if you cannot afford a sit-stand desk, a sit-stand adaptor can provide you with similar benefits of easing your muscles and improving your concentration by reducing tiredness levels.

QUICK TIP: *Stand up and stretch regularly. Sitting still for several hours will lead to muscular problems and increase your tiredness.*

▶ FOCUS ON YOUR EYES

Staring at your computer for hours on end is not good for your eyesight. Indeed, optometrists have a name for it, "computer vision syndrome" (CVS). This is caused by staring at the screen with a somewhat fixed glare for an extended period. As a result, the muscles of your eyes do not move very much, and your eye itself is fixing its focus in one position. The result is a combination of problems that together make up CVS. These include:

- Dry eyes
- Red irritated eyes
- Itchy eyes
- Eye discomfort
- Blurred vision
- Headaches.

As a student studying online, you could be more prone to CVS than a traditional university student as they will be spending less time just staring at their computer. All of your work is conducted staring at a computer, so you need to take special care of your eyes and prevent the problem of CVS from arising. The chances are very high that you will suffer from CVS. A study of university students found that 90 per cent of them had symptoms of CVS (Reddy et al., 2013).

Obviously, taking regular breaks, as outlined earlier, will help your eyes in addition to all the other benefits. Every time you take a break, you will stop staring at your screen, thereby giving your eyes a rest. However, there are other steps you can take. For example, you can buy special computer glasses. These are relatively cheap items that you can buy from online stores. They slightly magnify the screen for you, making it easier to see your work and reducing eyestrain. Research shows that the use of these glasses can help (Blehm et al., 2005). Another way you can help is by the use of lubricating eye drops or sprays. Again, you can buy these over the counter in many supermarkets or online. By using these drops or eyelid sprays several times a day, you can reduce the amount of dry eye, which appears to be fundamental to the production of CVS.

> QUICK TIP: If you wear spectacles or contact lenses, tell your optometrist that you will study online and use your computer for several hours a day. The optician may be able to provide you with a new prescription that will help reduce the chances of CVS.

▶ GET PLENTY OF QUALITY SLEEP

One of the problems with computer screens is that they transmit "blue light". This can have an impact on your eyes, by making them dryer, for example. Hence, problems such as CVS can be made worse because of the technology pushing out blue light towards your eyes. However, one of the main problems with the blue light that is emitted from computer screens is that it can cause your body clock to "misfire". The result is that your brain isn't quite sure when you should be sleeping. Too much blue light can disrupt your sleeping pattern. As an online student sitting in front of computers each day, you will get a considerable amount of blue light. So, there is a real risk of sleep disturbance when you study online.

Students have traditionally had some difficulties with sleep. It's not uncommon for students to get home in the middle of the night after being out with friends. Nor is it unusual for students to complain about lectures at 9:00 am since many of them are not even out of bed at that time of the morning. Disrupted sleep seems to go with the territory. Students appear to accept that abnormal sleep patterns are what is required to be a student. There's a view that you are not a proper student if you are not staying up late or hiding under the duvet until lunchtime. However, irregular sleep is a problem. In fact, research shows that if a student's sleep is regularly disturbed, they get lower marks overall (Hershner and Chervin, 2014). In other words, poor sleep can reduce your ability to get a good degree. To make sure that you get the best marks possible, you need to ensure that you get a good night's sleep on a regular basis.

To ensure you sleep well, minimising the impact of blue light is helpful. This is because the accumulation of repeated amounts of blue light fools your brain into believing it is daytime. As a result, the hormonal changes that prepare your body for sleep tend not to happen when you are subject to large amounts of blue light. When you go to bed, your brain still thinks it is daytime, and you find it difficult to get off to sleep. Therefore, reducing the amount of blue light you receive can help ensure sound sleep patterns. There are blue light filters and blue light spectacles you can buy. However, the evidence of their value is mixed. Some studies find a small benefit, whereas other studies haven't been able to demonstrate significant improvements due to these devices. You are welcome to try them, of course, to see if they do have any benefit for you. Just don't fall into the trap of believing they are the solution to the blue light and sleep problem.

The most beneficial method of getting good sleep is to go to bed at roughly the same time every night. It appears that your body clock gets used to the rhythm and arranges your sleep pattern effectively as a result. Going to bed at around the same time each night and getting up on a regular pattern each day appears to have the most significant impact on overall sleep. Of course, there will be occasions when you can't go to bed at the same time, but if you strive to almost always have the same bedtime, then you will find your sleep improves.

For online students, though, regular bedtimes can be a problem. The studying never goes away. Unlike campus-based students, where lectures appear on a timetable, the material for online studying is always there. As a result, it can be more difficult for those studying online to wind down at the end of the day. There is always the availability of the online materials, and it is easy to get engaged with some learning, meaning you go to bed late.

> **QUICK TIP: Have a cut off time for studying. Just because the study materials are always-on does not mean you have to be. Stop studying so that you can go to bed according to a routine.**

There is one other important reason for ensuring you do not allow excessive computer use to interfere with a good night's sleep. Research has shown that poor sleep quality is linked to stress and depression in university students (Ramos et al., 2021). Not getting good quality sleep can affect your mental health, which, in turn, can have an impact on your degree results.

▶ GET SUPPORT

Studying online can be lonely. Unlike traditional university students, where there is always someone in the kitchen or bar to talk to, those who study online often only have their families around them. Social support from friends and people in the same situation as ourselves, can be significant in terms of alleviating or preventing mental health issues. You may think that you have people to talk with at home. However, parents or siblings do not understand the situation you are experiencing as they are not doing the online studies. Other students will know what you are going through because they are in the same situation. On campus, all students are in similar situations, and so when they chat with each other about any issues or concerns they have, there is a shared understanding. For online students, alone apart from their family around them, there isn't anyone you can bump into who has that shared experience.

Universities will provide online students with the ability to be social. There will be "student-only" forums set up for you to use.

The Students' Union will also have online discussion groups in which you can take part. Whatever is offered, take advantage of it. However, research shows that the online social activity offered to students is not the same quality as face-to-face opportunities to socialise (Nicol, Minty, and Sinclair, 2003). Indeed, one of the points I make to my Open University students is that they should make attempts to meet each other in the real world, even if it is just to chat over a coffee. So, use the student online social system to locate other students who do not live too far away from you. You can then arrange to meet up with them in a coffee shop or bar, for instance. You don't need to be on the same course as all you are doing is just getting the support of others in the same situation as you. If you are concerned about your safety, meeting up with a stranger alone, then I would suggest that you only meet up in small groups of individuals in a place that is mutually convenient.

> QUICK TIP: Establish a support network of fellow online students so that you can help each other whenever struggles arise.

Keep in touch with Personal Tutors

All university students will be likely to have a "Personal Tutor". This is an academic who is there to help support you through your entire university career. They will help you with general academic issues. A Personal Tutor will also help you with your academic skills. Plus, Personal Tutors are there to help support you when you have personal issues or other difficulties.

Almost all lecturers will have a group of Personal Tutees they look after. They take the student through from arriving at university to graduation. However, not all students take advantage of the Personal Tutor schemes. I have checked with my colleagues, and we all tend to find that about one-third of our Personal Tutees make regular contact and seek support throughout their time at university. Another third of students only occasionally seek our assistance, often at a time of some difficulty or an emergency. Then there is a final group of students who never approach their Personal Tutors and never respond to meeting requests. This is a shame because it appears that some of these students struggle with a variety of difficulties but do not seek the help that is available to them.

Because online students have limited support available to them at home, forming a good relationship with a tutor will be of significant help. So, at the outset of your studies, make sure you get in touch with your Personal Tutor and maintain that relationship throughout your degree. You will be able to get plenty of help and advice, making your study at a distance more manageable and more enjoyable. In fact, research shows that the provision of tutors for online students is a critical component in helping them learn (McPherson and Nunes, 2004). While this research was considering subject-specific learning, it does point the way to the fact that distance learning students benefit from a relationship with academics. It shows you cannot just "get on with it" when studying online. It is worthwhile accepting from the outset that you need the support of your Personal Tutor so that you can use the system to its full advantage.

> QUICK TIP: Get in touch with your Personal Tutor at the outset of your studies and stay in touch throughout your degree.

Use the university well-being department

Every university has a well-being department. It might have another name, such as Student Support or Student Services, but there is always a team of people available to provide students with a range of support. This can range from physical and mental health issues to personal problems, relationship breakdowns, and disputes with friends. These well-being departments have counsellors, therapists, and specialists who can help support students with special needs such as dyslexia or ADHD (Attention Deficit Hyperactivity Disorder). Whatever this department is called at your university, make use of it. They are there to help. For students on campus, they can just walk into the well-being department. Where I work, the well-being team is located right next door to the main academic building at the centre of campus. When I was a student, the well-being department was halfway between the middle of campus and the student accommodation area. However, for online students, there is no accessible drop-in centre that is visible. Online students need to make a special effort to find the well-being department's online access. Make sure you know how you can get in touch with the well-being team and never be anxious or concerned about contacting them. There is no judgement made about you, just a desire to help.

> **QUICK TIP:** *Make a "bookmark" of the well-being department's web page or online access. That way, you can be sure you can contact them easily when you need to do so.*

There is one other very important reason for being in touch with the well-being support team. Suppose something happens and you find it difficult to complete your assignments. In that case, you will be permitted to make a plea for mitigating circumstances. In this situation, the lecturers can give you extensions or defer your assessment, depending on what happened. When students submit claims for mitigating circumstances, one of the checks generally made is with the well-being team. No confidential information is shared; the well-being team will just confirm that they know the student and their situation. This means that the plea for mitigation is more likely to be accepted. However, when a student says they have been having personal problems that prevent them from completing an assignment, but the well-being team are unaware of this, then getting an extension is more difficult for the student as they may need to provide evidence for particular issues. If you are in contact with the well-being team, such evidence is often unnecessary. Hence, being in touch with well-being support workers can help ensure that your case for mitigation is easier to process.

▶ ONE FINAL IDEA – HOUSEPLANTS

Get some indoor plants for your study space. Computers do not help the air quality of your home. Indeed, having a computer in your room is roughly equivalent to having three other people in the same space. Research on rooms with computers shows that the reduction in the air quality can reduce typing performance (Bakó-Biró et al., 2002). Studying online, particularly with a computer in your bedroom, means that the air quality of the room can decrease. To help overcome this problem, it is a good idea to get some indoor plants. Research has shown that when students were asked to complete cognitive tasks in an office where there were plants, their performance was improved compared with those asked to do the task with no plants present (Raanaas et al., 2011).

> QUICK TIP: *Tall green foliage plants are thought to help your concentration, so getting a couple of these in your study room could help improve your work.*

PRACTICAL TIPS

- **Establish a routine for breaks.** Take regular breaks where you get up from your desk. These will help you maintain concentration, improve memory, and help your eyesight. Stand up, move about, and stretch your muscles. If you use the Pomodoro Technique®, you can do this after each 25-minute block of work.
- **Use a desk.** It might sound straightforward, but many students appear to try to study with a laptop perched on their knee or even while lying down in bed. Sitting at a desk improves your posture and reduces the chances of muscular problems. Plus, it helps you focus and concentrate.
- **Take care of your eyes.** You will be doing a lot of work at your computer, and it can help increase dryness in your eyes. To help deal with this, use lubricating eye drops regularly so that you can reduce the chances of CVS.
- **Get regular sleep.** Try to go to bed at the same time each night and get up at the same time each morning. This will help settle

your body into a routine that will minimise the impact that using computers can have on sleep patterns.
- **Use the support systems.** There is plenty of support available for online students. This includes student-only social forums, Personal Tutors, and the university's well-being or support team. Make sure you know how to contact these services and make use of them. You are studying alone at a distance, and it is therefore expected that you will want additional support.

▶ REFERENCES

Asundi, K., Odell, D., Luce, A. and Dennerlein, J.T. (2010) 'Notebook Computer Use on a Desk, Lap and Lap Support: Effects on Posture, Performance and Comfort', *Ergonomics*, 53(1), pp. 74–82.

Bakó-Biró, Z., Wargocki, P., Weschler, C. and Fanger, P.O. (2002) 'Personal Computers Pollute Indoor Air: Effects on Perceived Air Quality, SBS Symptoms and Productivity in Offices', in *Proceedings: Indoor Air 2002*, pp. 249–254. Herndon, VA: International Society of Indoor Air Quality and Climate.

Blehm, C., Vishnu, S., Khattak, A., Mitra, S. and Yee, R.W. (2005) 'Computer Vision Syndrome: A Review', *Survey of Ophthalmology*, 50(3), pp. 253–262.

Health and Safety Executive (n.d.) Work Routine and Breaks – Display Screen Equipment, Working Safely with Display Screen Equipment. Available at: www.hse.gov.uk/msd/dse/work-routine.htm (Accessed: 6 November 2021).

Hershner, S.D. and Chervin, R.D. (2014) 'Causes and Consequences of Sleepiness among College Students', *Nature and Science of Sleep*, 6, pp. 73–84.

Kowalsky, R.J., Perdomo, S.J., Taormina, J.M., Kline, C.E., Hergenroeder, A.L., Balzer, J.R., Jakicic, J.M. and Gibbs, B.B. (2018) 'Effect of Using a Sit-Stand Desk on Ratings of Discomfort, Fatigue, and Sleepiness Across a Simulated Workday in Overweight and Obese Adults', *Journal of Physical Activity and Health*, 15(10), pp. 788–794.

McPherson, M.A. and Nunes, J.M.B. (2004) 'The Role of Tutors as an Integral Part of Online Learning Support', *European Journal of Open and Distance Learning*. Available at: www.eurodl.org/materials/contrib/2004/Maggie_MsP.html (Accessed: 15 August 2021).

Nicol, D., Minty, I. and Sinclair, C. (2003) 'The Social Dimensions of Online Learning', *Innovations in Education and Teaching International*, 40(3), pp. 270–280.

Osama, M., Ali, S. and Malik, R.J. (2018) 'Posture Related Musculoskeletal Discomfort and Its Association with Computer Use among University Students', *Journal of the Pakistan Medical Association*, 68(4), pp. 639–641.

Park, J.H., Moon, J.H., Kim, H.J., Kong, M.H. and Oh, Y.H. (2020) 'Sedentary Lifestyle: Overview of Updated Evidence of Potential Health Risks', *Korean Journal of Family Medicine*, 41(6), pp. 365–373.

Pragier, E. (1986) 'Work Breaks for Keyboard Operators', *Australian Journal of Physiotherapy*, 32(3), pp. 157–160.

Raanaas, R.K., Evensen, K.H., Rich, D., Sjøstrøm, G. and Patil, G. (2011) 'Benefits of Indoor Plants on Attention Capacity in an Office Setting', *Journal of Environmental Psychology*, 31(1), pp. 99–105.

Ramos, J.N., Muraro, A.P., Nogueira, P.S., Ferreira, M.G. and Rodrigues, P.R.M. (2021) 'Poor Sleep Quality, Excessive Daytime Sleepiness and Association with Mental Health in College Students', *Annals of Human Biology*, 58(5), pp. 1–7.

Reddy, S.C., Low, C.K., Lim, Y.P., Low, L.L., Mardina, F. and Nursaleha, M.P. (2013) 'Computer Vision Syndrome: A Study of Knowledge and Practices in University Students', *Nepalese Journal of Ophthalmology*, 5(2), pp. 161–168.

World Health Organization (2002) 'Physical Inactivity, a Leading Cause of Disease and Disability, Warns WHO', World Health Organization. Available at: www.who.int/news/item/04-04-2002-physical-inactivity-a-leading-cause-of-disease-and-disability-warns-who (Accessed: 6 November 2021).

Useful resources

This is a list of some helpful online resources for anyone studying online.

▶ STUDYING ONLINE

This is the website I have created to accompany this book, which has
several lists of resources, software and apps, all kept up-to-date.
https://studyingonline.tips

▶ THE STUDENT SURVIVAL SKILLS HUB

A collection of useful resources for students from the publishers of
Studying Online, Routledge.
www.routledge.com/our-customers/students

▶ GET STARTED WITH ONLINE LEARNING

This is a free course from OpenLearn, part of the Open University, on
how to start learning online.
www.open.edu/openlearn/education-development/get-started-online-
learning/content-section-overview

▶ UCAS STUDY SKILLS GUIDES

A series of guides from the UK University and Colleges Admissions Service (UCAS).
www.ucas.com/undergraduate/student-life/study-skills-guides

▶ THE RAPID E-LEARNING BLOG

A useful blog that is regularly updated with information about learning
   online.
https://blogs.articulate.com/rapid-elearning

Index